MW00626240

Letters to My Unborn Children

"In his thoughtful and personable *Letters to My Unborn Children*, Shawn fulfills the silent prayer of every bereaved parent: to discover the strength, courage and hope within ourselves that allows us to carry on in a way that honors the children we lost."

David Fleming, ESPN
Author of *Noah's Rainbow: A Father's Emotional Journey from the Death of His Son to the Birth of His Daughter*

"Although this book is written for anyone whose heart has been devastated by the loss of a pregnancy, I loved hearing Shawn's perspective as a grieving father. Shawn's handling of grief in his book is both skillful and thoughtful because he refuses to further injure…or insult…his readers with simplistic solutions to very painful and complex questions. I recommend this book for people who are tired of feeling alone in their suffering."

Rev. Dr. Alex Gee, Fountain of Life Church, Madison WI
Author of *When God Lets You Down,* and fellow grieving father of two prematurely born daughters

"*Letters to My Unborn Children* eloquently conveys Shawn's passage from raw grief to acceptance and hope following the multiple miscarriages that he and his wife experienced. Shawn shares how his faith and interactions with others throughout his life shaped his reactions to loss and made him who he is today. Insightful, courageous, and sensitive, this is a superb resource for families living through the pain of miscarriage."

Tim Nelson, A Place to Remember
http://www.aplacetoremember.com
Author of *A Guide for Fathers: When Your Baby Dies*

"We have rituals, traditions and experience to help us know what to do and how to feel when the life of someone we love ends, even if in youth. But we know much less about what to do and how to feel when a life we have only begun to love ends just as it is starting. *Letters to My Unborn Children* can help. Shawn weaves together wise and compassionate words from writers, song writers and Scripture with his own honest probings. His deeply felt and thought-filled reflections on the heartbreak of miscarriage cast comfort and light on the pain of any loss."

Dr. Daniel Taylor, Bethel University
Author of *The Myth of Certainty:*
The Reflective Christian and the Risk of Commitment

"*Letters to My Unborn Children* is a powerful, starkly honest, and deeply moving account of what happens when darkest grief is acknowledged and explored rather than denied and shunned. Shawn names the deeper, more invisible losses of his specific grief. His insights offer both comfort and encouragement that invite others to acknowledge their own stories of loss. A powerful read."

Ruth E. Van Reken
Author of *Letters Never Sent: A Global Nomad's Journey from Hurt to Healing* and co-founder of *Families in Global Transition*
http://www.figt.org

"*Letters to My Unborn Children* is moving, eloquent, deeply Christian, and unfailingly honest. Parents who have suffered through miscarriage will find that it gives words to their thoughts and feelings. Indeed, it gives words to the thoughts and feelings of anyone who has suffered the death of someone they loved."

Dr. Nicholas Wolterstorff, Yale University
Author of *Lament for a Son*

Letters to My Unborn Children

Meditations on the Silent Grief of Miscarriage

Shawn T. Collins

Huff Publishing Associates/
Quill House Publishers

MINNEAPOLIS

LETTERS TO MY UNBORN CHILDREN
Meditations on the Silent Grief of Miscarriage

Copyright © 2012 by Shawn T. Collins.

Library of Congress Cataloguing-in-Publication Data
Collins, Shawn T.
Letters to My Unborn Children: Meditations on the
Silent Grief of Miscarriage / Shawn T. Collins.
 p. cm.
Includes bibliographical references.
ISBN 978-1-933794-58-7

Quill House Publishers
Publishing consultant: Huff Publishing Associates, LLC
Cover design by Daniel Netkin-Collins, www.dncdesign.org
Front cover photograph by Ahmed Al-Shukaili, www.sxc.hu/photo/1009358
Interior design by Marti Naughton

DEDICATION

To my three unborn children.

To Kristine. My companion in this
journey of silent grief.

To Elise, Charis, and Clare. Participants with me
in the extreme sport called parenting.

With hope for the day when we will all meet
on that beautiful shore.

CONTENTS

1

APRIL 2004–SEPTEMBER 2004

Letter to My First Child

The Pregnancy

Dear Child,

Your arrival was very unexpected news for us twelve weeks ago. Your mother and I have never been good at making rapid decisions together. We are both meticulous, and prone to worry about uncertainty. The prospect of parenthood plays into both of those, because it's very uncertain and not at all meticulous. We could never get past approaching it with a mixture of hopes, dreams, and fears—hopes and dreams as we watched some friends enter this stage of life; fears because of the glaring weaknesses in our characters, and concerns about our ability to be good parents. We found out about you on a Friday morning when your mom had the day off work. My first reaction was to burst out laughing. I told your mom it was evidence of a Divine sense of humor.

Here we were, two undecided fearful people being given the title of parents before we even knew for sure we wanted it! I'm sure God was smiling at us.

That Sunday I drove into church for an evening service of Compline. This monastic service ends the day by placing yourself into God's hands through chanted prayer. It is one of my favorite parts of attending our church. Part way into town, out of the blue my stomach quivered and I cracked a huge grin as I thought, *"I'm going to be a dad!"* For a brief moment, some of the excitement I'd been trying to keep under wraps broke through my fear in a visible way.

The day before, I'd gone skiing with two friends. I found myself watching the families with young children quite a bit. I enjoyed watching the kids bounce up and down off the snow. I'll admit to a twinge of jealousy that they were so much better at 5 or 6 than I was at 27. I think the biggest thing that struck me was how much the activity of skiing was clearly recreational for both parents and young kids. I've heard people say *"Have fun before you have kids because you won't afterwards when you're tied down."* I didn't get the sense that was the case on the slopes, though. I found that encouraging as I thought about other activities we enjoy that we could include you in.

Drawing on our mutual science training, mine in engineering and your mom's in pharmacy, we looked at what was going on in her body as a complex experiment. Framing it that way helped me see the changes in your mom as something to enjoy, rather than something to be intimidated by. We started changing our diet to get the right nutrients for the two of you, and tracked your growth from pictures in a pregnancy book. We'd keep tabs on her body to try and see what changes the pregnancy was initiating. She helped me see this as a biological version of extreme sports. She was very excited to see what her body would do. She made me excited to watch.

The emotional changes are harder to describe, but were more fun to watch. Over the last couple years as I'd watched her interact with children of our friends, I'd had a growing conviction that she would be a good mother. She usually disagreed with me, mostly because she felt so inadequate. But she had started to acknowledge a desire to be a mother. The pregnancy legitimized her desire and dream of motherhood, and took credence away from some of her fears. The dream grew in her, taking shape in things like talking to you while she jogged, telling you how much she loved you and looked forward to meeting you.

You came into our lives at a time when many other things were in turmoil. Right after we found out about you, there was a particularly nasty series of events in the world news, including a story about mothers and orphans coming out of the Rwanda genocide. Deployment of a new computer system at the hospital had your mom working long, generally tense, hours. Several issues came up within my immediate family that highlighted long-standing relational tensions and destructive behavior patterns. At one point, my prayer in response to these issues was to say *"God, I think it's not right that my blood should be passed to another generation."*

In the midst of this there were times we wondered what we were doing bringing a child into such a broken world. How could we in good conscience willingly give you life when many aspects of that life were so clearly rotten and painful? To these questions, the pregnancy was also a source of hope. As I have struggled with my faith in recent years, one growing conviction has been the importance of a God who is active in human history. Rather than giving us a way to escape the world, we see God entering the world in Christ, taking suffering on himself so that this broken world can be healed. To follow Christ is to refuse to give up being actively involved in the world, and to deliberately act in faith that God remains present in this dark world. Your life was a symbol of that hope for us. A contemporary poet, Calvin Miller, said every baby is evidence God still dreams of Eden.[1]

Mingling with this hope and anticipation, I often felt afraid and frustrated. Some of this was selfishness. I had a set of tasks and activities planned for this year— taking a heavy summer course load to finish my Master's degree in Mechanical Engineering, joining a band in the fall to play trombone for the first time in many years, possibly taking a field support position in Spain with my job during the fall. These were exciting things for me personally, and there were times I was frustrated at the prospect of having to give them up. In particular, I didn't want to trade these areas of competence for pregnancy and fatherhood, which I viewed as areas of uncertainty, inexperience, and incompetence.

Some of this was also fear. For many years now, relating to other people is something I have found quite terrifying, and consequently difficult to participate in. At times I craft the great narrative of my life as that of a misfit. I am a freak who does not fit in because of my height, my reserve, academic and personal interests that rarely overlap with those of people I interact with. That freakishness means I am clumsy at best when I interact with other people. In particular I am clumsy when I have not rehearsed, if necessary written down beforehand, the items of discussion. Somewhere in my youth or adolescence a powerful voice lodged in my head with a message that *"You may interact with others when you are competent. You may never make them pay the price for your imperfection."*

When I listen to that voice I become very afraid of interaction. I tend to retreat inside myself. Babies are a major fear source, partly because of my glaring inexperience. Combine that with fear that my 6'5" frame would inflict physical damage on someone so much smaller than me, and someone (you) who needs feedback from a father (me) who rarely visibly emotes. All this adds up to say it is not right that someone suffer the experience of being my child. This fear, more than the frustration at potential changes to tentative schedules, was the major source of uncertainty as I thought about meeting you.

Again, the pregnancy was a source of hope in the midst of my fear. It became a call from God to accept the relational risk of parenthood, to deliberately choose to honor a set of hopes and dreams I have kept as deep secrets, and to deliberately choose not to honor the fear that drives so much of my relational life. So I began to pray for you, silently at first then out loud with your mom. Mostly it was the Old Testament Aaronic blessing that concluded our wedding liturgy.

"Lord, please bless and keep my child. Make your face shine on this child and be gracious to him or her. Lord, please lift up your countenance upon my child, look with favor on him or her, and grant him or her peace." It was a nightly prayer made with my hand on your mom's belly and head—the closest I could get to coupling the prayer with physical contact as I prayed for both of you.

As this happened some of my other dreams began to take shape as well. I started looking for strollers we could use to take you jogging and biking, and thinking about where we could start swimming lessons. A longer term, perhaps deeper desire was to find ways to share with you a love of instrumental music that had resurfaced for me in recent years. I also began thinking about how to share the news of your expectation, particularly with my family when I saw them at the end of April. I could tell my brother we'd picked a birthday present for him— the title uncle. I could tell my mom, a week before Mother's day, to add a new title—grandmother. I'd ask my sister to route her return from Kenya in December through Hartford. I'd tell another brother I had an excuse for him to visit us. These were each celebrations I anticipated eagerly.

The Miscarriage

The day before Easter we had friends from church over for a Seder dinner to celebrate the Passover. Your mom and I remembered our first Seder at Purdue in 1998, before we started dating. I had asked her to light the candles and read the opening prayer. That request

was one of the early signs to her that I was interested
in more than friendship. For this dinner in 2004, we
conspired to secretly give her non-alcoholic wine.
I was excited that we'd kept this secret for 9 weeks,
and were only 3 weeks from breaking the news.

Unknown to me, your mom started spotting blood
that day. The next day, after discussion with her parents,
we decided to see the doctor as soon as possible.
Although your mom was worried, at the time I didn't
think it would be anything serious. Ignorance is bliss,
and the previous 9 weeks had been very hassle-free.
The first sign of a problem was Monday when the
ultrasound showed a sac only 5 weeks old. We knew
this was wrong. Based on the calendar and your mom's
cycle, the sac should have been 9 weeks old. They asked
us to come back that Friday for another ultrasound.
The doctor told us that spontaneous miscarriages
occur 20% of the time under normal circumstances.
She stressed the fact that it couldn't be linked to
something we'd done, or to stress from your mom's
job. As prone to self-criticism as we are, I think we
needed that verbal message: *"Shawn and Kristine, you
have not done anything wrong. You cannot legitimately
blame yourselves for this."*

It is difficult to describe what the next week was like.
I had a set of work and school activities that occupied
most of my waking hours. For the most part I think I
was just in a state of shock. I refused to believe you were
dead. I maintained a skeptical, *"We'll see what happens."*
attitude. This was hard on your mom, who understood
that the ultrasound meant you were probably dead.
She was ready to process the miscarriage, and I refused

to acknowledge it. This made our interaction very tense. It was worse because there was nothing either of us could do but count the hours. It was just awful. I called my dad Monday night to say, *"Dad, the good news is you were a grandfather even though you didn't know it. The bad news is you're probably not anymore, but we really don't know."* He prayed with me on the phone, confessing faith in a God who controlled the miracle of life, and consequently in whose hands the miscarriage was still only a possibility at the time.

Friday we went in for the second ultrasound. The sac showed no growth, confirming the miscarriage. The nurse gave us some time alone in the exam room before we went next door to see the doctor. I don't remember much. I held your mom, who shed a few tears, and then we went to the doctor's office. The doctor reiterated the message from Monday—this happens under perfectly normal conditions, often from unknown causes. It was not because of anything we did or did not do.

As we left the office, there was a young lady there in tears. We think she'd just found out she was pregnant. It is an ugly law of un-grace that we encountered. One couple in tears because they'd lost a child they wanted; one girl in tears because she'd been given a child she didn't want. It just was not fair. It was hard not to be both bitter and jealous.

Driving away, we decided that maybe our jealousy was misplaced. While we would take a pregnancy in a heartbeat, would we truly want a pregnancy in the context where it would be undesired? Is it better to weep alone than to weep together knowing we would soon be fully supported by both of our families? The emotion of jealousy was easy to experience, but hard to justify in that light.

In some ways, after so much uncertainty that week, the miscarriage was a relief. Had the news been positive, we would have been concerned about health of mom and baby given a six week sac that should be ten weeks. Now, we had freedom to begin grieving. Your mom went for a long run after she dropped me off at work. It was welcome after a week of being sedentary for fear of hurting you.

I called my family over the next couple days. I think my parents expected the news because of my call earlier that week. My siblings were pretty surprised. I don't know which shock was greater—the news of the miscarriage or the news of the pregnancy! For them, as for us a few weeks earlier, you were an unexpected presence.

The church service that Easter Sunday was one of the most difficult I've ever had to participate in. The Lutheran liturgy during the Easter season is filled with words of celebration. It rejoices in life, in Christ's resurrection, and in His victory over death. The opening prayer, the hymns, and the Creed all celebrated this life that is so central to the Gospel message. As I participated in the liturgy, every fiber of my being cried out in protest. *How can we celebrate life when my child has died? How can you people of this church celebrate life today? Don't you know that my child is dead?* There was tremendous dissonance for me. You were our miracle child—the gift God knew we wanted but were afraid to ask for. Now that miracle had been taken away, and I was supposed to celebrate God's victory over death? Hearing others speak the liturgy of victory drew tears of grief. I stumbled several times as those tears prevented me from saying the words myself.

The next week was full of activities again. I was finishing the semester and preparing for a conference in New Orleans. Your mom was preparing for a three week trip to be the matron of honor in a friend's wedding, watch her brother graduate from college, and attend a pharmacy conference. I remember very little deliberate processing of grief. Mostly we just tried to survive.

Thursday was a hard night for your mom. She had severe cramps, and passed several blood clots. Friday morning we asked the doctor if a dilation and curettage (D&C) was still necessary. He recommended it as a safety measure to avoid an emergency room trip in a strange city later. When I talked with him on the phone after the surgery, he told me the decision had been wise. There was still material to be removed from your mom's uterus. He said she did very well during the procedure and that he expected her to recover. She looked much better when I saw her after she woke up. She was alert and cheerfully talking with the nurses to get details about her medications. She said she felt much better now that the D&C was done. After watching her misery Thursday night, I was relieved to see her so alert and cheerful.

Grieving

With the D&C done, travel preparations complete, and semester over, I finally found space to begin grieving. I have wrestled with several dimensions of this. What is it your mom and I have lost? Where do we say you are in the realm of the afterlife? How does, or should, our identities and outlook on life change?

I think we lost two things. The first is the miraculous gift of your conception. That unexpected life was lost. People say we can have more children. That is probably true. But we didn't want children in the abstract. We wanted a specific child—you—the special gift and source of hope in the midst of life that was so chaotic. Your life and all it meant to us cannot be replaced. I never dreamt of being a husband. In fact for much of my life I did not expect to be a husband. But in a specific time and place I met your mother. Through her love I found the courage to become the husband of a specific person—Kristine Collins. Four years later your presence in our lives gave us the strength to become parents of the child conceived in February, who we would meet in November. I grieve the loss of the specific child who helped me start this new journey.

Second, I grieve the loss of all that we were anticipating. This journey from fear to hope—can it continue or did it end with your death? We have not been to New Hampshire since we moved to Connecticut. We planned to visit this fall so that we could walk on the trails and see the leaves changing colors. We joked of being far enough along in the pregnancy that your mom would be my "waddling wife." We will not make that trip to New Hampshire this fall so I can take my waddling wife on trails to see the leaves.

The loss of what might have been is difficult because it is so abstract, but I think characterizes the pangs of grief that I have felt. We both fought tears in the airport after the D&C as we saw people with small children, especially babies. There was a young mother and her son on my flight back from New Orleans. Sharing the flight with them made the journey a time of mourning for me. *"That would have been me in a few months, but it will not be."* The pangs are not as sharp as they used to be. I still feel them periodically—in the supermarket seeing babies in carts, discovering a co-worker is expecting his first child, hearing a former roommate and his wife are expecting in October. It is generally the more anonymous conditions that hurt. In anonymity I can watch and grieve. In relationship I am juggling my grief with celebration for the other, which is hard.

One thing I hope you will know is that we never considered the idea of not grieving. Your death was, and is, the loss of a real person. One of your mom's friends said she shouldn't cry because the loss was too early to have been a real baby. We appreciate her desire to comfort us, but we disagree. Both positions are statements of faith. We will live in faith that you were, and are, a real person.

Where you are in the afterlife is perhaps better stated as what is the role our faith has played in all this? Putting the vast fragments of thoughts that have gone through my head in the last couple months is a monumental task. Making them coherent is even more so. Many of these thoughts took shape as I read and re-read Nicholas Wolterstorff's *Lament for a Son.* It records his grief during the year after his son died in a mountain climbing accident. I shed many tears reading that book in the weeks following the D&C. Sometimes I could not complete passages I'd try to read aloud to your mom without crying.

There are a couple things about Wolterstorff that I appreciate. The first is his willingness to admit confusion. He doesn't try to define an answer—God has a deliberate purpose in his son's death, or God couldn't do anything about it. He simply says, "I don't know." He doesn't try to "get over" his grief, nor does he allow his brooding to control him. He does strive to see the world in a new way.

> Looking back I see I was trying to own my grief. If you would know me, you will know that I am one who has lost a son. I have no explanation. I can do nothing else than endure in the face of this deepest and most painful of mysteries. To the most agonized question I have ever asked I do not know the answer. I do not know why God would watch him fall. I do not know why God would watch me wounded. I cannot even guess…My wound is an unanswered question. The wounds of all humanity are unanswered questions.[2]

My own confusion presents me with some unanswered questions. How do I pray for my loved ones—particularly your mom? I pray God will bless them, but that was my prayer for you. Death wasn't the blessing I sought for you. Is that the blessing they will get when I pray for them? If we get pregnant again do we tell people it's our first pregnancy?

I have changed, perhaps for the better. Your mom and I have grown closer together through this. To my earlier shrouded fear of lack of emotions, I found I have been able to grieve. I find I loved you a depth my fears wouldn't let me realize.

Was it worth it? I don't know. It is hard to say yes. I would trade those things in an instant to have your life back, to be expecting to meet you in a few months, and to have been able to continue that miraculous journey to fatherhood that was so cruelly cut short.

Wolterstorff draws on Psalm 42 to say that lament is the context in which faith endures.

> "Back and forth, lament and faith, faith and lament, each fastened to the other, a faith emptied of newness:
>
> As the deer pants for streams of water so
>   my soul pants for you, O God.
> My soul thirsts for God, for the living God
> When can I go and meet with God?
> Yet in the distance of endurance I form the song:
> By day the Lord directs his love, at night
> His song is with me—a prayer to the God of my life."[3]

I've struggled to grasp lament as a mode of faith since I first read Wolterstorff while I was in college. So much of my worldview is built around finding answers to things, including faith. My training in apologetics says there is no question to which the Christian tradition cannot provide an irrefutable answer. The lament says there are questions for which irrefutable answers are insufficient, perhaps irrelevant.

It is very tempting to try and explain all this away— I've just got to believe this was for the best, that God either did this or allowed it to happen for a reason. It is also tempting to take the other side and be consumed by self-pity because I've been the victim of such a terrible thing. The doctor said this happens to about 30% of pregnancies in our age group. If this is all about me and my experience of pain, the rest of the folks in that 30% group only matter because they're like me. They're made in my image, so they become important. That view is as flawed as it is blatantly self-centered. I am not the center of the universe. It seems wrong to interpret my life's events as though I am.

That said, I'm dissatisfied with the determinism that seeks to find the hand of God in your death. In the name of sovereignty, I think these explanations miss a recurring scriptural theme that death is the enemy, not the instrument of God. It was conquered at Christ's resurrection and will be overcome at his return. Until the overcoming is complete, death is a sign of the fallen world—evidence of the huge gap between what God intended and what is. To say otherwise is to refuse to acknowledge and where possible take responsibility for, the broken elements of the world that so frequently cause death.

More important than my brief lapse into fragmented theorizing, I was not, nor am I, really looking for an answer to the "Why?" Perhaps that will come some day. What I needed was a mechanism to express my confusion and grief. Knowing why it hurts doesn't change the fact that it hurts. Hence my earlier comment about the irrelevance of irrefutable answers.

Wolterstorff's lament created that space for me to mourn the awfulness of your death. Not as an angry shout at the futility of life in a world that burned me one too many times. Nor as blind acceptance of actions from a distant God whom I've no right to question. But to acknowledge the loss of a life I was growing to love, the end of a journey that hardly had a chance to begin, the absence of a relationship I was looking forward to entering. These things were important enough to radically alter the way I viewed the world for the five weeks I thought you were alive. Their loss should be important enough to alter the way I view the world after your death.

The lament created space for me to honor the value you brought to my life, verbalize the pain of your loss, and express the confusion of trying to come to terms with a side of life I didn't expect to encounter. That space to talk about how I cried for you, for what you would bring to my life, was infinitely more valuable than finding a cure for the pain of your death.

Reflecting

In *The Horse and His Boy*, Shasta finds out after spending a miserable night alone that Aslan walked beside him through the night and kept him from falling into a deep canyon. I think that silent presence is a picture of what my faith has been during the last few months. I have often felt alone and confused, especially early on. But looking back, I think I can see the hand of God. As I read *Lament for a Son* over and over; as we received self-conscious, anxious comfort from two friends at church; when a couple co-workers said to your mom, *"I also had a miscarriage. It is an awful thing and I will help you in any way I can;"* when my sister sent a note saying, *"Please know that you are loved;"* as your mom and I cried on each other's shoulders. Each of these moments gave me strength to keep going. I think they helped me out of the canyon of anger and despair. I am still confused, and I periodically feel pangs of grief. I am not angry, and I think I'm not bitter.

I come at last to the question of what has changed. The first change was my relationship with your mom. A level of reserve between us disappeared on our honeymoon when we changed from engaged couple to husband and wife. Another level of reserve disappeared when we found out she was pregnant. This change initially baffled both of us. The explanation we settled on was a shift in perspective from "This is my spouse" to "This is the parent of my child." Neither of us has much personal self-confidence in our ability to be parents, but we were both convinced the other person would be a good parent. We were excited to see each other enter that role.

One somewhat surprising thing is that in general the pregnancy did not make me afraid of fatherhood. I wrote earlier about my concerns, and my feeling that it would be cruel to make anyone suffer from being my child. I also had a hidden hope. I think it began in 1995 when I first met my two youngest siblings, who my parents adopted while I was in college. It grew later as I watched some friends from church become parents. Those experiences had kindled hope that instead of being a paralyzing experience, interacting with young children could be something I enjoyed. Since both hope and fear are abstract, many times for me the fear is the more powerful abstraction. The pregnancy put a concrete focus on the hope that made it more powerful. As that happened I found I was not afraid as I'd expected to be, nor as my track record of need for control would have predicted. Many times I've held back from young kids—partly from fear of them because they're so much smaller than I am, partly because other folks just tend to get there first. For example kids are attention magnets at church, and I'm typically in the back of the crowd. I had a sense of reassurance from the knowledge that *"With this one I've got first dibs."* That may have also translated into being more at ease with small kids now than I was before, because it could have been me in their parents' shoes. I was much more comfortable than I have been in the past when a co-worker and his wife came for lunch with their 1 year old, and when we visited the other friends in September with their 1 and 3 year olds.

In *Lament for a Son*, Wolterstorff talks about owning his grief redemptively. It is part of his identity, not a flaw to be "fixed." This should provide an enlarged capacity to share in humanity's sufferings, to mourn more deeply and cry out at the brokenness of the world that so desperately needs redemption. I don't know if this has happened for me or not. Characteristically, much of my grieving has been solitary. I shed my tears over the pages of this letter, alone in my hotel in New Orleans, and during discussions with your mom after the D&C. There has been healing just in finding I am able to grieve. I don't know if I've become more open to those around me in terms of sharing my life or being willing to share theirs. I guess time will tell whether that change should, or will, happen.

Farewell

Here I am in early October, completing a letter begun at the end of April. It has been a long process of reflection, and somewhat humorous for your mom to observe how drawn out it has become. I hope you will see from these words that I really wanted to meet you. I was afraid and uncertain, especially early on, but there was a hope and anticipation that grew. I looked forward to meeting you and learning about this extreme sport called parenthood. I am very deeply sorry that you died so early into this strange journey we began together. No trite answer, theological, biological, or otherwise, will ever change that.

I will close with two texts that were especially meaningful to me during the week after the D&C. The first is a gospel song of farewell that I originally heard on Selah's *Press On* album. I've changed the words to come from a father to his child rather than between friends. The second comes from the funeral service in the *Book of Common Prayer*. I used this prayer to release you into God's hands when we came home after the D&C.

Now you've come to the end of life's journey
It turns out we'll never meet anymore
Till we gather in heaven's bright city
Far away on that beautiful shore.
Since we'll never get to meet this side of heaven
As we struggle through this world and its strife.
There's another meeting place somewhere in heaven
By the beautiful river of life
Where the charming roses bloom forever
And separations come no more
Since we'll never get to meet this side of heaven
I will meet you on that beautiful shore.[4]

Into your hands, O merciful Savior, I commend my unborn child. Acknowledge, I pray you, a sheep of your own fold, a lamb of your own flock, a sinner of your own redeeming. Receive this child into the arms of your abiding mercy, into the rest of your everlasting peace, into the glorious company of those who dwell in your light. And may your kingdom of peace come quickly. Amen.

Farewell, Child, until we meet face to face for the first time. Go with my love.

Dad

2

LAMENT

On the Death of My Second Child

Kristine miscarried a second time shortly after we found out she was pregnant again. I knew that I wanted to write a letter to my second child. I could not find any words of my own. In the aftermath of the second D&C, I desperately needed a mechanism to express my grief and confusion. I didn't need something to help me express how much Kristine and I were hurting, or to answer the "where-is-God" question. I just needed something to help me say "*This is really, really rotten. It stinks.*" It stinks so much because it's the loss of hope that I tried so hard to build during the three uncertain weeks when we knew Kristine was pregnant. And it stinks because the dream of parenthood that grew with those two pregnancies also lies in pieces at my feet, perhaps beyond reach forever.

I had previously experienced this inability to speak during a time of isolation as an undergraduate student. My mother e-mailed me a reflection on the New Testament story of Jesus healing the paralytic. She pointed out that the man was healed, in large part because of the faith of his friends who were willing to carry him to Jesus. She encouraged me that my parents' love and prayers would carry me to Christ during this time of isolation when I wasn't sure what to say or think. In the aftermath of the second miscarriage, I was again the wounded man on the mat. I had to be carried by the faith of others. That faith was expressed in the words from Wolterstorff's requiem, which began my own lament.

REQUIEM—Nicholas and Claire Wolterstorff[1]

Truly terrible is the mystery of death
I lament at the sight of the beauty
Created for us in the image of God
Which he's now in the grave
Without shape, without glory, without consideration
What is this mystery that surrounds us?
Why are we delivered up to decay?
Why are we bound to death?
John of Damascus

Like a bird alone in the desert
Or an owl in a ruined house
I lie awake and I groan
Like a sparrow lost on a roof
Ashes are the bread that I eat
I mingle my tears with my drink
    Psalm 102

From the depths I cry to you, O Lord
Give heed to my lament.
    Psalm 130

I was comforted after the first miscarriage by the idea that beyond giving apologetically sound theodicies, God grieves with us when we grieve. This is the progression in Wolterstorff's Requiem. The next sections talk about Christ as the suffering servant, and then of the hope that the resurrection brings. I was trying to move myself through the same progression. Having written how much the miscarriages hurt, I tried to reflect on my own mortality and then find hope in the resurrection.

REQUIEM—Nicholas and Claire Wolterstorff[2]

In all our afflictions he is afflicted
and the angel of his presence saves us;
in his love and pity he redeems us;
he lifts us up and carries us all our days.
>   Isaiah 63:9

He bears our griefs
and carries our sorrows;
by his wounds we are healed.
>   Isaiah 53:4, 5

Though the fig trees do not blossom
nor fruit be on the vine;
the produce of the olive fail
and the fields yield no food;
though the flock be cut off from the fold
and there be no herd in the stalls,
yet will I rejoice in the Lord;
I will joy in the God of my salvation.
>   Habakkuk 3

We have seen a great mystery:
We shall all be changed.
We shall be raised in Christ
as we were buried in Christ.
Death is swallowed up in victory.
The dwelling of God will be with his people.
God will wipe every tear from their eyes;
and death shall be no more.
There shall be no mourning, no crying nor pain;
sorrow and sighing shall flee away.
For the old things are disappearing.
>   Revelation 21

Wolterstorff helped me say that the miscarriages were ugly. But the message of hope in his Requiem wasn't enough. Perhaps I wasn't able to hear it. I couldn't reconcile my conflicting emotions. In the midst of the uncertainty before the miscarriage I had often felt resignation and despair. Had I given up too soon? Could I have done more to try and love my second child during those three uncertain weeks? Could I have done more to comfort and support Kristine, and so avoid our frequently tense discussions? I still needed a voice for my confusion. Rich Mullins gave me this voice by helping me say simply that *"I do not understand what is happening."*

HARD TO GET[3]

You who live in heaven–hear the prayers of those of us who live on earth. Who are afraid of being left by those we love and who get hardened by the hurt. Do you remember when you lived down here where we all scrape to find the faith to ask for daily bread. Did you forget about us after you had flown away? Well I memorized every word you said. Still I'm so scared I'm holding my breath while you're up there just playing hard to get.

You who live in radiance–hear the prayers of those of us who live in skin. We have a love that's not as perfect as yours was–still we do love now and then. Did you ever know loneliness–did you ever know need? Do you remember just how long a night can get when you are barely holding on and your friends fall asleep, and don't see the blood that's running in your sweat? Will those who mourn be left uncomforted while you're up there just playing hard to get?

I know you bore our sorrows. I know you feel our pain. I know it would not hurt any less even if it could be explained. I know I am only lashing out at the One who loves me most. And after I have figured this, somehow all I really need to know is if you who live in eternity hear the prayers of those of us who live in time?

We can't see what's ahead and we cannot get free of what we've
left behind. I'm reeling from these voices that keep screaming in
my ears. All these words of shame and doubt, blame and regret.
I can't see how you're leading me unless you led me here where
I'm lost enough to let myself be led. And so you've been here all
along I guess. It's just your ways and you are just plain hard to get.

I think that more than anything else, I just wanted to
forget. The broken dreams of parenthood. The tension with
Kristine before the miscarriage became final. The fact that
even in the midst of growing hope of parenthood, there
were times I didn't want to become a father. The question
of whether I could have, or should have, loved more during
the uncertainty of the second miscarriage. Even though
I knew there were positive things that happened during
both pregnancies, their memories hurt too much. I didn't
want to remember them.

David Adam helped me face this pain. Wolterstorff's
reflections on the suffering servant offered hope because
there was a time in the past when Christ suffered. Adam
offered something different. He gave the image of Christ
walking with me in the present, through the conflicted
experiences of this miscarriage. He gave the image of Christ
physically underneath me, lifting me up from the despair
and confusion that weighed me down. The story of Aslan
in my first letter provided an image of Christ beside me,
keeping me out of the valley of despair. Adam's images
of Christ underneath me stopping me from sinking, and
before me helping me move forward gave me the courage
to remember again.

CHRIST BEFORE ME[4]

Christ, you enter through the door of the past with
Your love and forgiveness.
You can come where doors are closed and bring light and peace.
Christ, I put my hands in Yours, for I am afraid;
I bring memories that hurt and a past that pains,
for Your healing and renewal.
Christ, come enter through the door of the past;
Into the remembered and the forgotten,

> Into the joys and sorrows,
> Into the recording room of memories,
> Into the secret room of sin,
> Into the hidden room of shame,
> Into the mourning room of sorrow,
> Into the bright room of love,
> Into the joyful room of achievement.

Christ, come enter

> Into the fabric of my being
> Into the conscious and subconscious
> Into the roots of personality.

Cleans me from secret faults and renew a right spirit within me.

CHRIST BENEATH ME[5]

Christ, no matter how far I have fallen, You are there
also; 'Underneath are the everlasting arms,'
Christ, I look at the hands that uphold me and I see the print
of nails. The hands that bear me up know pain and sorrow.
You, Lord, know the betrayals and rejections of this world.
Christ, 'if I descend into hell You are there also.' You experienced
the many hells of this world. You have descended so that You
can lift us up. In all dangers, You are there to support us:

> In the storms of life,
> In the sinking of the disciple,
> In the scorning and rejecting,
> In the betrayals and denials,
> In the hells and crucifixions,
> In the ebbing out of life,
> Christ beneath me.
> And I know that You are the Risen Lord of Life.

Adam gave me the strength to remember. Buechner helped me turn that decision to remember into something tangible. I was choosing to remember more than just the positive changes that took place in me. I was also choosing to remember the lives of the two children Kristine and I had lost. Remembering granted them dignity. Granting them dignity both encouraged and challenged me to continue the journey from fear to hope that the two pregnancies helped me begin. It also gave me the strength I needed to write the letter to my second child, for which I'd previously had no words.

REMEMBER[6]

When you remember me, it means that you have carried something of who I am with you, that I have left some mark of who I am on who you are. It means that you can summon me back to your mind even though countless years and miles may stand between us. It means that if we meet again, you will know me. It means that even after I die, you can still see my face and hear my voice and speak to me in your heart.

For as long as you remember me, I am never entirely lost. When I'm feeling most ghost-like, it's your remembering me that helps remind me that I actually exist. When I'm feeling sad, it's my consolation. When I'm feeling happy, it's part of why I feel that way.

If you forget me, one of the ways I remember who I am will be gone. If you forget me, part of who I am will be gone.

"Jesus, remember me when you come into your kingdom," the good thief said from his cross (Luke 23:4). There are perhaps no more human words in all of Scripture, no prayer we can pray so well.

3

OCTOBER 2004–JANUARY 2005

Letter to My Second Child

The Pregnancy

Dear Child,

It is almost one month since the D&C formalized your death, just one month after we'd learned of your life. The delay is partly due to busyness. It also reflects the turmoil in my mind that makes writing coherently a difficult thing. One reason for the lament before this letter is that I've relied on the words of others to express my feelings. I needed that freedom from the need to innovate with words in the midst of a crisis. Nevertheless here I am now, writing my letter of welcome and farewell to you.

We found out about you on Sept 1, the day before leaving for a ten day vacation in Maine. The news was more of a confirmed suspicion than a surprise. Your mom had been feeling physically unwell for a week with a bunch of symptoms that made me suspect she might be pregnant. Although we hadn't talked about it, she had also wondered the same thing. The pregnancy test confirmed her suspicion, as her news to me at the dinner table confirmed mine.

We both met the news with mixed emotions. There was the excitement at the news of your life, mingled with the concern that we would have another miscarriage, mingled with physical and mental exhaustion that made it hard to react at all. Cautious hope is probably the best way to describe our thoughts—wanting to believe but not sure the news was real.

The next day we started the two day trip north to Baxter State Park. The park is a large wildlife preserve in northern Maine, where we planned to tent camp for five nights, then overnight backpack for two nights. We spent the first night just outside Portland. We arrived around 7:30, and were so tired we were in bed and asleep by 8:00. Looking back, I'm not clear on all the reasons for the exhaustion. The summer had been draining for me as I wrapped up my M. S. degree in Mechanical Engineering at Rensselaer. Not in a bad way, but just taking up a good deal of time and energy. There was also the normal toll of preparing for the trip, and the early pregnancy queasiness and exhaustion. Finally there was the physical toll from our fear that the pregnancy would end prematurely.

When we got to Baxter State Park I felt a little like I was at one of the many parks I grew up visiting in Kenya. I have fond memories of the camping trips with my family to different national parks in Kenya. It was familiar and comforting to drive for an hour on a dirt road to a campsite with no running water, where we had to pack our garbage out when we left. Again we were in bed early—in part from exhaustion, in part because our habit when we camp is to go to bed soon after sundown.

Over the next couple days, some of our fear and exhaustion began to recede as we enjoyed the quiet and serenity of the park. Saturday we hiked Doubletop Mountain: a roughly 4 mile trek on a trail that connected with our campground. Sunday we went the other direction from the campground, walking part of a trail toward a campsite we planned to be at for our last two nights. Monday we climbed Mt. Katahdin via the nine-mile round trip trek that included completing the final portion of the Appalachian Trail. Tuesday we put folding chairs out by the river and spent the day reading. I took advantage of a couple natural water slides and played in the river for a few minutes. Very cold, but quite fun. And it got your mom and me laughing with each other.

During these days, we discussed what would happen if the pregnancy went full term. We figured you'd be born in April, around one year from the first D&C. Your mom's four month maternity leave would last through the summer. That would let us take an extended vacation to introduce you to friends and family at a time when time off at the hospital where she worked was generally quite scarce.

We tried to figure out how many weeks we were into the pregnancy, so that we had an idea when we could start telling people we were expecting. I had a couple dates in October in mind to make

the announcement—a previously planned party
with friends and coworkers to celebrate finishing
my degree at Rensselaer, a rendezvous with some
extended family when they were in town, or sending
my mom a birthday card on October 11 telling her
something like, "Happy Birthday Grandma." We
decided that each of these events was before the
twelve weeks in the first trimester finished at the
end of October. That meant they were too early to
be celebratory announcements of the pregnancy.

One thing we discussed several times was being
able to tell stories of what we did in Baxter while your
mom was pregnant. I wanted to get an infant-sized
t-shirt made saying, "I climbed Katahdin." We took
collective pride, and your mom took personal pride
in the thought that she was doing this wilderness
experience of camping and hiking as a pregnant woman.

Through these chats there was a sense of hope
that began to build. It was cautious, because we feared
the possibility of miscarriage, but some expectations
began to form. We were able to say that *"We really
would like to meet this child. These are some of the
things from Baxter that we will remember if we do."*

The Miscarriage

Wednesday we were supposed to break camp and
begin a two-day backpacking trip. The weather forecast
predicted two days of rain from remnants of a hurricane
that had just hit Florida. We changed our plans and got
an empty cabin at Kidney Pond. The weather cleared up
enough that we took a short hike up a nearby mountain
for lunch. After the hike we began unloading the car. On

one trip from the cabin to the car, I passed your mom going the other way. I could tell something was not right. When I got back from the car, she was in tears on the cabin porch. She told me she had started spotting again.

We didn't think the spotting guaranteed a miscarriage. Even though we knew it wasn't always a sign of problems, it was hard not to assume the worst. How grateful, in a strange way, we were that the rain had changed our plans, and that we'd been able to get into a cabin. Had this happened at the end of a long day backpacking with 7 miles of rough terrain between us and the car, the situation would have been considerably worse. As it was we had a place of physical shelter where we could rest for a day before heading home.

We spent Thursday, a very wet and rainy day, inside—reading in our cabin and in the camp lodge. Your mom had a stack of Tin-Tin comics and a couple Harry Potter books. I had a cognitive anthropology text to read for the first course toward my PhD in Anthropology. I should note with humor that this apparent discrepancy in material is quite common when we read together. She has "fluff" material while I have "academic" material. It is actually an excuse for me to read over her shoulder. This time I read most of the material I brought. I also skimmed most of books three and four of Harry Potter during our week in Maine.

Friday we drove south to Portland. We spent Saturday browsing shops in Freeport. A highlight was finding a small store selling British trade goods, including Bournville and Marmite. Bournville is a dark chocolate bar made by Cadbury. Marmite is a dark spread that goes on toast. Both are rare and

expensive in the U. S. They were staples of my diet
growing up in Kenya. Like Baxter providing a sense
of the familiar, the Bournville and Marmite gave me
cherished foods that I could celebrate getting to buy.
The Marmite also provided humor for your mom
and me. She firmly believes it is completely inedible.
It was helpful to have something to laugh about.

Despite much that was pleasant during these three
days, we could not escape a cloud of uncertainty. There
were a couple different elements that went into this.
One was a feeling that we were repeating a cycle—the
miscarriage was inevitable so we should prepare for it.
Another was a feeling that we didn't want the same story
to occur, and that we would do anything within our
power to fight for you to live. Despite this desire, we felt
helpless because we realized that probably the outcome
of life or death couldn't be impacted by anything we did.
Lastly, there was a sense of anger and confusion, sort of
*"I understand that it's normal for this to happen once, but
why twice, and why to us? It's not fair."* That mixture of
fear and frustration was very difficult to shake during
the whole process. It definitely took its toll on us.

When we got home we decided to try and get
another ultrasound right away. We were somewhat
uncertain about this because spotting in early
pregnancy can be perfectly normal. In fact, had
spotting not been the early warning sign of the first
miscarriage, we might not have been concerned. Your
mom had an ultrasound that Tuesday (September
14). The results showed a live sac with a heartbeat
of about 80 beats per minute, not the expected 120
beats per minute. This was cause for both hope

and concern. Hope because you were alive. Concern because the low heart rate was an early warning sign of a likely miscarriage. We had another ultrasound the next Monday (September 20). The results were the same. The sac had grown, but the heart was beating slowly. Again, we had the mix of hope and concern.

That ultrasound was a strange experience for me. It's one thing to watch what's going on when they're confirming death. It's another thing to watch when they're looking for signs of life. I tried very hard to pick up the signs the technician was using to make her diagnosis. The sac looked to me like a light gray outline on a darker gray background—not an easy thing for your color-challenged father to follow evidence on. The most amazing thing was seeing the blips of light on the screen that showed your heart beating. I talked with my dad that night about the "wonders of the womb" and my sense of awe at getting to glimpse the miracle of new life growing, even in this uncertain state.

The next ultrasound, on September 27, confirmed the miscarriage. There was no heart beat, and the sac was starting to break up. We scheduled the D&C for that Thursday so your mom would have four days to recover before going back to work.

Reflecting

A couple phone conversations during these days played an important role in how I experienced this miscarriage. My mom encouraged us that although we could not control the physical outcome of what happened, our decision how to react would have a significant impact on how we experienced the next few weeks. She told us we needed to find reasons to laugh, to keep our hopes up, and to refuse to believe your death was inevitable. This became a recurring theme over the next few weeks of uncertainty, although it was easier said than done. We were trying hard not to be weighed down by the fear, but often felt very burdened and uncertain. Our thought process was something like:

EVENT→INTERPRET IN FEAR→ANALYZE→
FIND CAUSE FOR HOPE→TRY TO TEMPER FEAR WITH HOPE→
VOICE MIXED FEELINGS.

My mom's thought process was more like:

EVENT→INTERPRET IN HOPE→VOICE EXCITEMENT.

My dad took the stories of the ultrasound, and reflected on how amazing the process of new life forming—the wonders of the womb—and how amazing it was to get a glimpse of that life through the medium of ultrasound technology. I experienced the ultrasound as giving some hope that mostly reinforced a need for concern. He experienced it in wonder as the gift of a glimpse into the miraculous formation of new life that was taking place.

I cannot understate how much I appreciated their efforts to be so excited and hopeful during this time. What fears they had they did not share. This helped them play a vital part in strengthening us in the midst of our own fear and struggles to function.

Another discussion was with my brother Gregory, between the 1st and 2nd ultrasounds. His question, " *Have you thought more about the kids thing?*" elicited two responses. The first was some of my thoughts from the first pregnancy and miscarriage. The key elements were our decision to accept uncertainty, lack of control, and lack of predictability as inherent parts of pregnancy and parenthood—things to be celebrated rather than avoided. We had come to see pregnancy and parenthood as something of an extreme sport: an experience that would have us in over our heads, where we probably didn't know what we were getting into, but something we wanted to approach and enjoy as uncertain, rather than tie ourselves in knots by trying to bound it into something we could control. This allowed us to identify things we would look forward to if the miscarriage didn't occur. The Katahdin t-shirt was a small example.

The other thing we discussed was the idea that someone observing your mom and I could interpret our lives as somewhat idyllic. We have degrees from a good school, are a fiscally sound dual-income-no-kids (DINK) household, claim to be genuinely happy in our marriage, etc. etc. Gregory told me in 2003 that "*You guys are approaching sainthood in our minds.*" He and I have discussed this in the past. I contend this external "perfection" occurs in the context of turmoil and uncertainty, often significant, and almost always not observed. My reticence has a lot do with this, coupled with geographic distribution in my family that tends to restrict information flow.

What we talked about specifically here was the glaring dissonance of repeat miscarriage and our so-called idyllic life. Put simply, people who do everything right don't have pregnancy loss, do they? This dissonance caused some turmoil for your mom and me. Not that we don't expect failure, but in the past we've been able to over-come early shortfalls through a mix of stubbornness, determination and hard work. Here we were faced with something we wanted—parenthood—something that prevented us from getting there—miscarriage—and absolutely nothing we could do or control to close that gap. Your mom and I have acknowledged our inability to completely control our lives in the past, but it's easy to develop a working assumption that we could manage the important areas. This was an important area that we couldn't manage. That was difficult to come to grips with. The phone call with Gregory was valuable in helping me voice some of that confusion.

I'll confess that part of me wants to throw this experience in the face of the next person who says my life is a success, or that I don't mess up. Even if that person is me. It's sort of the bitter trump card to play as evidence that looks can be deceiving.

One thing your mom and I discussed many times was the pain of wanting something—lack of miscarriage, but really a healthy pregnancy and birth—and the helplessness of not being able to do anything to bring it about. We were helpless during the time of uncertainty while we waited to find out if you were going to die. We were helpless again when the miscarriage was confirmed. In the face of this helplessness our first reaction was to exert more control, to treat your life as something we were entitled to, and to hold God responsible for granting us our dues in the form of a healthy pregnancy. We decided that the way we treated this uncertainty before the miscarriage would set a big precedent for how we treated uncertainty as parents. We could make the tight-fisted claim on your life now—we'll only love you if you don't die on us, or we could hold your life with an open hand and offer our love unconditionally. All this had very little to do with what happened when the uncertainty was over. It was primarily about how we chose to approach your life regardless of what happened.

I re-read *Till We Have Faces* during these discussions, because I knew its themes were similar to what we were discussing. In the book, C. S. Lewis tells the myth of Cupid and Psyche from the perspective of Psyche's older sister. During a conversation with the widow of a deceased advisor, the widow offers this explanation for why she didn't stop her husband from working himself to death in the sister's service.

> "Keep him to myself at what cost? Make him mine so that he is no longer his?"

> "And yet, he would have been yours."

> "But I would be his. I was his wife, not his doxy. He was my husband, not my house-dog. He was to live the life he thought best and fittest for a great man—not that which would most pleasure me. You have taken [my son] too. He will turn his back on his mother's house more and more; he will seek strange lands, and be occupied with matters I don't understand, and go where I can't follow, and be daily less mine—more his own and the world's. Do you think I'd lift up my little finger if lifting it would stop it?[1]

Near the end of the book she lodges a complaint against the gods for taking Psyche from her. It reads (in part) as follows:

> "The girl was mine. What right had you to steal her away into your dreadful heights? ... I was my own and Psyche was mine and no one had any right to her. Oh, you'll say that you took her away into bliss and joy such as I could never give her, and I ought to have been glad for her sake. Why? What should I care for some horrible, new happiness which separated

her from me? Do you think I wanted her to be happy that way? Did you ever remember whose the girl was? She was mine. Mine. Do you know what the word means? MINE!"[2]

My bedtime reading during this period came from Soren Kierkegaard in *Devotional Classics* by Richard Foster. Part of it reads:

> "Lord! Make [my] heart your temple in which You live. Grant that every impure thought, every earthly desire might be like the idol Dagon—each morning broken at the feet of the Ark of the Covenant. Teach [me] to master flesh and blood and let this mastery of [myself] be [my] bloody sacrifice in order that [I] might be able to say with the Apostle: I die every day."[3]

We saw that parenthood in general, and this pregnancy in specific, was becoming something about which we would say, *"Our life is incomplete without this."* In that sense it was like Dagon—a false god that claimed our allegiance and defined the way we reacted to the events of our life. And our love for you, such as it was, was the possessive consuming love of Psyche's sister.

In *With Open Hands*, Henri Nouwen talks about prayer being a process where our fists become unclenched and their contents are released into God's care. A focus of my prayers during this time, both when I was with your mom and while I biked to and from work, was the admission how tightly clenched our hands were around this pregnancy, and the request that God pry our fingers open. Not that we wanted to be open-handed about this—we didn't. But if we weren't, we would pay the cost for trying to control and regulate something that was out of our hands.

The release was only partial, but the process of recognizing it needed to happen was important. Over

Thanksgiving we talked with one of my college room-
mates and his wife about the idea that *"Lord, when
I agreed to follow you by faith, I didn't sign up for this
(repeat pregnancy loss for us; infertility for them) to have
repeat pregnancy loss."* Although I still feel that way,
I've gone through another iteration of recognizing that
I can't live the life of faith on my terms. The pain of
your death is no less keen, but the bitterness and anger
that simmered during the weeks of uncertainty were
significantly reduced as I went through that iteration.

  Devotional Classics also contains a private prayer
regimen written by George Buttrick. Several of these
steps were important for me in my biking/praying
routine going to and from work. They helped me
work through that process of opening up my hands.

> WIDESPREAD MERCY: "There is an ingratitude
> in human nature by which we notice the black
> disfigurement and ignore the widespread mercy. We need
> deliberately to call to mind the joys of our journey."[4]

I needed this exhortation because the miscarriage
was a blot that wanted to be the focal stain of our lives.
The 45 minute morning bike ride to work gave me a
chance to reflect on and acknowledge the "joys in the
journey": the peace of the back road cycle commute,
the physical health that let me travel by bike, the Prius
we'd get in October, all the help during the uncertainty
before the D&C—hours on the phone with my parents,
Gregory and his wife, the kindness and care of the folks
at the obstetrician's office, the love of and for your mom.
Those times of thanksgiving on my bike were important
in helping me mentally balance the darkness of your
death with gratitude for significant goodness in my life.

CONFESSION: "our sin is against the Living Order, and we have neither inward peace nor inward power until we have offered prayers of penitence."[5]

CONTRITION: "the wise prayer of confession always leads to an acceptance of God's pardon…It might be wise to rise to symbolize both our resolve to make wise restoration insofar as we have power to mind our blunders and our sincere renunciation of our sins…our will, however feeble it may be, must descend squarely on the side of new life."[6]

Your mom and I had many difficult discussions during that period of uncertainty. *Why is this happening again? Should we assume the worst or hope for the best? How can we be hopeful when the evidence from the slow heart rate is so clear? Is it fair to this child to refuse to acknowledge its life before the uncertainty is resolved? Why is God absent in that He hasn't prevented this death? Don't we deserve better than this? By what right do we say the only evidence of God's action is a healthy pregnancy? Why is life unfair? Many who don't want children have them and many who want children can't have them. If we remove the assumption that life is fair and that we are among those for whom the result of that fairness is happiness and health, then what exactly is it we should be expecting?*

None of these are easy questions to ponder in the best of circumstances, and certainly not in the worse of cases. There were times I was frustrated and impatient with your mom: for her tears; for asking different questions than mine; for asking the same questions and getting different answers; for being a part (even unwillingly) of a situation I'd never willingly choose.

The exhortation to confess created space for me to acknowledge the frustration with your mom, and the place that my own wrongdoing had in those feeling. Following

Buttrick's sequence, I combined my prayers of confession, *"Lord, forgive me for my frustration at my wife"* with contrition, *"Lord, help me to be patient with her, to love her, to support her during this time of uncertainty."*

> INTERCESSION: "Intercession is more than specific: it is pondered: it requires us to bear on our heart the burden of those for whom we pray. It is also daring—it carries on its heart-entreaty the crisis of the world."[7]

Buttrick says intercession begins with those with whom we're embittered. With the confession of frustration, my intercession began with your mom. Using Buttrick's words: *"Lord, bless my wife whom I have wronged by my frustration. Keep her in your favor. Banish the bitterness I have felt with her."* I prayed that she would have strength to fight the fear and cynicism, and that she would have strength to endure the trial of uncertainty, and that I would find ways to show her love and support.

> PETITION: "Sometimes, in sorrow, dread, or helplessness, it will be a crisis cry of creaturehood—a beating on heaven's door with bruised knuckles in the dark…Yet it should always acknowledge that our sight is dim and that our purposes are mixed in motive."[8]

My petitions felt very much like the bruised knuckles beating on heaven's door, as I prayed for your life. I acknowledged that the odds were slim based on the visits to the doctor. Nonetheless I told God how much your mom and I wanted your life. I knew it was a potentially dangerous desire—partially wrapped up in the devouring love and desire for control I talked about earlier. So I made this prayer with its fallibility and mixed motives, the tightly coupled healthy and unhealthy desires placed before the throne of God.

This was a change from the first days of early warning signs. My initial reaction had been a sort of bitter resignation—Here we go again, why do we try when this is the result, and what good does it do to do anything but assume the worst? Through the discussions with your mom and miles of prayer on the bike, that changed as I saw some of the dangerous assumptions we held and began to see our hope for your life not to end. This did not take away the pain of your death, but by tempering some of the bitterness it allowed for (I think) a more healthy grieving when your death finally got confirmed.

Grieving

We did the D&C on September 30th so your mom would have Thursday-Saturday off work to recover. Many of the steps felt routine this time. We went to the same medical facility because we had appreciated their care the first time. Nevertheless I couldn't shake a feeling of dread that hung over me as we drove in, and as I left to grab breakfast during the surgery. I knew this was a routine procedure but I kept waiting to be told something had gone wrong and she was dead.

The bad news didn't come, and it wasn't long before they called me downstairs because she was awake. There was something in the first D&C—maybe the element of novelty—that enabled a degree of liveliness in our experience. Hence things like quizzing the nurses about your mom's medications. None of that was there this time. What I remember most is just a feeling of being drained. Neither of us said much. I sat and held her hand while we waited for the anesthesia to wear off enough for her to come to the car with me. We drove home, climbed into bed, and slept for several hours.

That feeling of being drained hung over me for many months after the D&C. Everything had happened so fast it was hard to react, much less process it all. The hope, fear, and chaos all overlapped during the month of September. As soon as the D&C was done, much of our time and energy was spent processing the rapid cancer development in your mom's grandfather (he died shortly before Thanksgiving). The whole month of October was a haze where I was unable to concentrate on either work or school. I don't think I began to feel mentally alert until we got back from our Christmas visit to Indiana. The three days with my in-laws and subsequent week off work played a big part in that.

One thing that came up early, and didn't get much attention, was the idea that your death was not just a loss to your mom and me. Our parents lost a grandchild; our siblings lost a niece or nephew. The day I told my dad the miscarriage was confirmed I gave him permission, with discretion, to share the news with others as he saw fit. That was the first time I realized my parents' experience of these events had dimensions other than their support of us.

I don't remember feeling intense grief as much as this dazed immobility punctuated by points of dissonance. Maybe much of the grieving was done before the D&C, during the phone calls and cycling I've already recorded. One Sunday shortly after the D&C, we were looking at the faith "Hall of Fame" in Hebrews 11. "By faith Abraham, even though he was past age—and Sarah herself was barren—was enabled to become a father because he considered him faithful who had made the promise." The teacher's point from the verse was an encouragement to maintain obedience, prayer and faith during the times of life's barrenness, as Abraham and Sarah had done. I told him afterwards that it was both pertinent and painful. Pertinent because the exhortation to endure rather than despair was true. Painful because we were hearing the exhortation in the context our own barrenness and death.

The same day, Pastor Corgan preached on the parable of the unjust judge who grants the widow her request because of her stubborn refusal to stop asking. Christ's message in the text: If an unjust judge is just because of this woman's stubbornness, how much greater will God's gifts be to those who ask. Pastor Corgan's exhortation: Be persistent and stubborn in prayer. If Sunday School was a knife getting stabbed into my gut, the sermon was the knife getting twisted while it was in there. Despite our prayers, and the prayers of those close to us, you had died. The justice we requested (if it could be called justice) had not been granted. So while we could not argue the truth of the text, it served to reinforce the brokenness of our life rather than heal it.

We found Thanksgiving to be very dissonant. This festival that celebrates family gathering and the abundance of life reinforced much of our grief. Again, the stabbing twisting dagger. Our first child should have been born mid-November, so it was very much a time of mourning. We deliberately chose not to celebrate Thanksgiving as one way of reducing that dissonance. It is not that we denied the many things for which we were grateful. But the process of reflecting emphasized the void caused by the deaths of our two children.

Christmas was also difficult for me. The family gatherings, gift exchanges, and celebration of Christ's new birth were painful reminders of the first birth that did not happen in 2004, the second birth that would not happen in 2005, and the related gifts celebrating a new phase of life that wouldn't be exchanged. As with the first Sunday after Easter, the celebration of new life in the church festivals produced a great deal of discord for me. *"How am I supposed to celebrate life when death has taken my two children? I don't deny the ultimate triumph that Christ's birth brings, but here and now, death is a big part of my world."* On Christmas Eve, the one song I appreciated was the Gospel hymn, "Sweet Little Jesus Boy."

> The world treat you mean Lord.
> It treat me mean too.
> But please sir, forgive us Lord.
> We didn't know it was you.

The idea that Christmas is a time of lament and mourning was new to me, yet it makes some sense. If we celebrate Christ's coming to bring redemption and restoration of relationship, it is legitimate to acknowledge how far the world currently is from that redeemed state. Perhaps it wasn't such a bad time to reflect on the broken world Christ lived in, the broken world we live in now, and the desperate need for healing.

My brother-in-law said a church in Lafayette holds something like a "Service of Mourning" every year at Christmas, specifically for those who have lost loved ones. I wish I'd known about it in advance. That is something I would have liked to attend.

In working through a class project on organizational decision-making, I found quite a bit of evidence for a systematic tendency to ignore warning signs of risk before catastrophes occurred. I think there is a significant parallel between this and the lack of discussion about pregnancy loss despite how common it is. There's some sort of embedded cognitive tendency to ignore what we can't understand, especially when it challenges an existing paradigm of how the world works. I spent many hours corresponding with a colleague about this, and how it shows up where we work.

A program was cancelled last year and now is almost stigmatized in discussion. After a few hours talking with the folks from that program, I found that they were struggling with many of the emotions I experienced during the miscarriages. There was much that was good they wanted to celebrate. There was bad they wanted to identify so it wouldn't happen again. There were factors out of their control that they wanted to identify so that they weren't held wrongly responsible (by themselves or others) for them. They felt the systematic silence about their project was negatively impacting the way our company functions now.

Celebrations of small successful projects were painful reminders of the many people whose hard work was ignored when this program was cancelled. We called these the *Rituals of the Silent*. We pondered what a ritual, or set of rituals designed to legitimize the space of experience of these silent grievers could look like. Perhaps these dialogues and explorations will be one place where I can respond to Wolterstorff's challenge to own my grief redemptively through an increased sharing in humanity's suffering.

Farewell

Here I am in January concluding the letter begun in October. I hope you will see from these pages of convoluted writing that we did want to meet you. We were afraid, uncertain, and often confused, but there were elements of hope and anticipation. I am very sorry you didn't get to wear the "I climbed Katahdin" shirt. Let me close once again with the song of farewell and the prayer of release.

> Now you've come to the end of life's journey
> It turns out we'll never meet anymore
> Till we gather in heaven's bright city
> Far away on that beautiful shore.
> Since we'll never get to meet this side of heaven
> As we struggle through this world and its strife.
> There's another meeting place somewhere in heaven
> By the beautiful river of life
> Where the charming roses bloom forever
> And separations come no more
> Since we'll never get to meet this side of heaven
> I will meet you on that beautiful shore.[9]

> Into your hands, O merciful Savior, I commend my unborn child. Acknowledge, I pray you, a sheep of your own fold, a lamb of your own flock, a sinner of your own redeeming. Receive this child into the arms of your abiding mercy, into the rest of your everlasting peace, into the glorious company of those who dwell in your light. And may your kingdom of peace come quickly. Amen.

Farewell, Child, until we meet face to face for the first time. Go with my love.

Dad

4

— —

LAMENT

On the Death of My Fifth Child

Kristine and I had two healthy girls after the second miscarriage. Elise was born in 2005, and Charis was born in 2008. When we decided to try and get pregnant again in 2009, I thought the first two miscarriages had prepared me for the possibility of a third miscarriage. The miscarriage happened on March 8, 2010. It was less than a week after Kristine brought home dinner from Chipotle to celebrate finding out from the doctor that she was seven weeks pregnant.

Unlike the first two miscarriages, which each stretched over three weeks, everything finished in less than forty-eight hours. We decided not to see the doctor when Kristine started spotting Sunday morning. She had spotted with all four previous pregnancies, and she was already scheduled for an OBGYN appointment in another week. We knew that an ultrasound would most likely give us instructions to come back for our scheduled appointment the next week. On Monday morning the spotting was heavy enough that Kristine arranged for an ultrasound that afternoon. The miscarriage was complete by the time we saw the OBGYN. No further surgery was needed. Kristine drove home while I picked Elise and Charis up from their daycare. The three of us stopped at Little Caesar's to get pizza for dinner. This was a monthly routine for our family, so the girls didn't know anything was wrong. For Kristine and me, the pizza freed us from having to think about dinner.

The letters I wrote to our first two children were important ways to name both my hopes for the pregnancies, and my grief after the miscarriages. With the third miscarriage, everything happened so fast that I wasn't able to write a full letter. The song at the end of this chapter became my lament as I searched for a way to articulate my grief and despair. A caim, or encircling, prayer, is a way to symbolize God's encircling love and protection. Some Christians pray a caim prayer while forming a circle around the person being prayed for. In a sense, they physically signify the love and protection they are asking God to provide for the vulnerable person in the center of the circle. The recurring "circle me Lord" prayers in the first part of the song used that symbolism to ask for protection from despair as Kristine and I committed to grieve the death of our fifth child together.

> This night, and every night, seems infinite with questions,
> And sleep as elusive as answers.
> Pain and longing are always present,
> Dulled just a bit by the day's distractions.
> I am weary.
> I am angry.
> I am confused.

Circle me Lord. Keep despair and disillusion without.
Bring a glimmer of hope within.
Circle me Lord. Keep nightmare without.
Bring moments of rest within.
Circle me Lord. Keep bitterness out.
Bring a sense of your presence within.[1]

I thought that Kristine and I knew the drill well enough that we could move past the initial surprise into actively talking about how to protect and nurture our family while we worked through the aftermath of the miscarriage. I was wrong. I was not prepared for the utter despair that settled over me after the doctor's appointment. I told a manager at work on Wednesday that

> After our first two miscarriages, I began to realize how many other places around me had similar patterns of hopes and silent grief. People started activities that carried possibilities for new life and associated hopes for the future. These dreams were often cruelly cut short for random reasons outside their control. I've worked hard to engage these areas in the last couple years: repairing fragmented department dynamics at work, encouraging people who work on cancelled programs or apparently fruitless efforts at global alignment that their hard work wasn't in vain.
>
> I've tried so hard to voice encouragement in these places because I want to see them as places where new life is growing. It has been a way for me to honor the lives of the two children we lost. Right now, I just want to give up. I don't know if I have it in me to hope for, or actively facilitate, that new life right now.

Pastor Dorsey's sermon that Sunday ended with a challenge that by responding to Gospel's call to enter the world, we find purpose, legitimacy, and meaning. I choked up while singing the Fanny Crosby hymn, "Hold thou my hand, the way is dark before me." At the end of the service, I couldn't sing the traditional spiritual, "you heal the sick and you raise the dead." Those tears helped me recognize my grief. I realized that I was responding to the miscarriage by completely withdrawing from the world. The words to my manager reflected a deeper emptiness which claimed my life wasn't worth living. The second part of the song, ending with the prayer to "lift me out of the valley of despair" voiced my cry that that emptiness would not be the last word.

> Tonight as on other nights, I am walking
>> alone through the valley of fear.
> O God I pray that you will hear me, for you
>> alone know what is in my heart.
> Lift me out of the valley of despair, and set my soul free.[2]

As I acknowledged that grief, the challenge from the sermon became clear. I could accept the narrative of darkness and despair that formed during the previous week. I could seek an alternative narrative which would help me live with hope and be an instrument of peace in the apparently fruitless areas I'd mentioned to my manager. The third part of the song was my prayer for strength to "walk the path I had never seen." As Kristine and I discussed that path, we committed to each other that the darkness of the miscarriages will not be the final answer that defines how they affect our lives. That commitment took shape through a final letter to all six of my children: Elise, Charis, Clare (who was born in 2011), and the three little ones who "we will meet on that beautiful shore."

> Bright King of heaven and Father Almighty,
> Make a roof for me by night, and guard me by day.
> If you are to bring me along the path I have never seen before,
> Make it a pathway for me to the life of glory.[3]

Caim Prayer - for Time of Grief and Loss

Text: Celtic Daily Prayer
© 2002 Northumbria Community
Music: Shawn Collins, 2010

5

JANUARY 2010–SEPTEMBER 2011

Letter to My Six Children

Dear Children,

Much has happened in the seven years since I wrote my letter after the second miscarriage. Elise was born in Connecticut in 2005. Your mom and I have completed the PhD journey that I began just before the second miscarriage, changed jobs, and moved from Connecticut to Indiana. Charis was born in Indiana in 2008. We had a third miscarriage in 2010. Clare was born in Indiana in 2011. Through these experiences we have continued to discuss the miscarriages–what went on at the time, how we each felt, how that impacted our grieving together, as well as how the miscarriages continue to shape the way we view the world.

Wolterstorff describes the isolation of grieving people from each other, and the toll that isolation takes on the relationship between the grievers. That certainly happened to your mom and I. We did not appreciate how differently we experienced the first two miscarriages. It has taken time for us to be able to compare notes about what

happened. That time for our minds and bodies
to recover has given us the space to see what we
weren't able to see in the middle of those crises.

I am writing this letter for two reasons. First,
I want to reflect with my unborn children on the
mixture of gift and grief that the three miscarriages
continue to be in our lives. Second, I want to reflect
with my living children on how they will grow up
seeing their parents engage the world in ways that
will always be shaped by their unborn siblings.

The Miscarriages in Our Worldview—
Seeking a Narrative

I wrote in the first letter about the miracle of your
conception. Part of that miracle was beginning a
phase of life that your mom and I were both afraid
to admit we wanted to enter. We had talked at length
between the two of us about the choice to have or not
have children. We had received comments (mostly
in jest) from coworkers who said parenthood was an
inevitable phase of life. We had received comments
(mostly serious) from family members who wanted
grandchildren, nieces, and nephews. My brother Deion
once prayed "*Dear Lord, please send Shawn and Kristine
a child in your own special time. And Lord, please make
that time be soon.*" Most importantly, I think, we had
watched close friends become parents. As we watched
them, and as we interacted with their children, we were
able to acknowledge our own dreams of parenthood.

These dreams meant that the first pregnancy was
not entirely a surprise. The timing was earlier than

we'd expected when we stopped using birth control. The dreams that emerged, although previously unspoken, were not new. In this context, there was a sense in which the miscarriage was a beautiful tragedy. Make no mistake—it was a tragedy, and it hurt. But the dream which emerged during the brief weeks of pregnancy was beautiful. We had time, even if only a few weeks, to discuss both our fears and our growing hope. When the miscarriage ultimately took place, we could view your lost life as something beautiful.

The second miscarriage was completely different for two reasons. First, we simply didn't have time for the dream to grow. There was less than a week between the positive pregnancy test and the bleeding that warned us something might be wrong. The miscarriage experience itself stretched out for almost three weeks between the early spotting and the final ultrasound. The total time we knew about the pregnancy was not much different from the first one—about four weeks. The first time, we spent those weeks building hopes and dreams. The second time, we spent them under a cloud of uncertainty and ultrasounds showing things were not right.

More importantly, we didn't have a paradigm to understand our experience. Our paradigm of solving problems through determination and perseverance could not explain our experience or equip us to go through it. On top of that, the repeated pregnancy loss forced us to face the possibility that we would not be able to have children. We had always assumed that if we decided to have children, we would have children. We weren't prepared for the possibility that parenthood was an unachievable dream. Your mom summed it up best during a conversation with me several years later, when she talked about her feelings of anger and vulnerability.

> After the second miscarriage, I was just mad. I was mad at God for not protecting a life that I wanted so badly. I was angry at you and others near to me because I needed support that none of you were able to give.
>
> I was also afraid. I wanted so badly to say that life isn't valuable only if it accomplishes something. Because if that's the case, it's not just a question of whether our unborn children were valuable. It's also a question of whether I'm personally valuable if I don't "do enough" with my life. When I couldn't find any value in the second miscarriage, it challenged that basic premise.
>
> Madeleine L'Engle (in <u>A Wind at the Door</u>) describes evil as this terrifying void of emptiness that you encounter. That's what I felt like the world became after the second miscarriage. I had this incredible sense of vulnerability as I realized just how much I can't protect myself or those I love from the pain of things like the miscarriages.

I said that we needed time to put our thoughts in order. As we discussed these feelings, we began to articulate that lack of a narrative. That helped us to understand just how painful it was for us as individuals, as well as the toll that it took on our marriage. We realized, as I've already written, that we had grieved and processed the first two miscarriages alone. We began searching for a narrative that we could share in our marriage, and that we could help our living children embody. We converged on the creation myth from Tolkien's *Simarillion*. In that myth, the creator, Iluvatar, equips the Ainur to sing for a theme he declared. Melkor, the character of evil, creates discord in the Ainur's music by attempting to create his own themes. Iluvatar responds to each element of discord by changing the theme the others sing. This goes back and forth until Iluvator ends the singing and shows the Ainur the world that their songs created.

> [Melkor] hath bethought him of bitter cold immoderate, and yet hath not destroyed the beauty of the fountains, nor of the clear pools. Behold the snow, and the cunning work of frost. Melkor hath devised heats and fire without restraint, and hath not dried up their desire nor utterly quelled the music of the sea. Behold rather the height and glory of the clouds, and the ever-changing mists; and listen to the fall of rain upon the Earth![1]

In claiming this narrative, we are choosing not to say that God planned the miscarriages, that we are grateful for them, or that we are better off for the experience. Most importantly, we will never say that our living children remove the pain of losing our unborn children. We will say that, like Iluvatar responded to Melkor's chaotic themes, we want to speak into the disharmony that the miscarriages represented by choosing to intentionally create things of beauty within the creative work of our own lives. But the beauty comes at the cost of the pain caused by the original discord and presence of evil.

The Miscarriages in Our Past and Present–Choosing to Remember

Part of embodying that narrative is our decision to remember the miscarriages. We will not try to forget them, or choose not to discuss them. Rather, we will allow present events (both joyful and sad) to trigger memories from the miscarriages. Those memories, although painful, have enabled some healing for us. Let me try and explain how this has taken shape.

We spent the Thanksgiving when Elise was about fifteen months old at our home in Connecticut. She had just started making the transition from crawler to toddler, and was beginning what became a rapid vocabulary expansion. We had nothing on our agenda for the day. Mostly, your mom and I watched Elise toddle through the living room and kitchen, put blocks into her plastic jar, and engage in various other activities that were common for her at the time. One of us realized part way through that morning that without the miscarriage two years earlier, Thanksgiving was about the time we had expected to meet our first child. We shed some tears together as we both remembered our loss and celebrated the little girl in front of us.

A similar thing happened about a year after Charis was born. I was holding her during a church service in April. As I reflected on the past year of her presence in our lives, I realized that our first miscarriage happened five years earlier. Four years earlier, we would have been getting ready to meet the baby whose life was ended by the second miscarriage. I whispered those two events to your mom. We shared some silent tears together as we remembered the miscarriages and celebrated the second little girl in my arms.

The remembering that I've just described is private or between your mom and myself alone. Another type of remembering occurs when we've chosen to tell others about our miscarriages.

Our pastor told us after the first miscarriage that while preparing to meet with us, he and his wife had discussed their own experience of miscarriage. Although it had been many years earlier, they shed tears together, and found it another step in their own healing process. That was my experience when a couple from our Bible study had a miscarriage shortly after telling us they were pregnant. I wrote them the brief e-mail below. The message took me about twenty minutes to compose, because every few words I would stop and cry. I was crying for our friends and their loss. I was also crying, once again, for the two children we had lost. Later that night I shed more tears as I prayed with your mom, saying *"Lord God, we grieve on behalf of our friends, because it is not right that this should happen."* And, like the comfort we found when coworkers said to your mom *"I've been through it, and it stinks,"* they were comforted when we shared our story.

> Dear Tricia and Nathan,
> We are very sorry to hear about your miscarriage. We also lost two babies during the first trimester before getting pregnant with Elise, so we can (sort of) sympathize with the transition from excitement to shock and grief. Losing our little ones was one of the most difficult chapters of our life. We are praying for each of you. I am also enclosing a portion of my journal, which was the brief liturgy of farewell I used with each loss. Again, you will be in our prayers.
>
> Dear Shawn and Kristine,
> Those liturgies of farewell are beautiful. Thank you for sharing them with us. I think I will print them and read them again as we go through this time of grief.

The second experience was with a coworker, Trevor. When he told us in the office that he and his wife were expecting, I heard him expressing many of the mixed emotions I had felt during our first pregnancy. Some time later, I asked when his wife was due. He said simply that "*she had a miscarriage.*" I went by his desk that day and said quietly that "*We had two miscarriages before our daughter was born. I don't know if I can be of any help, but I wanted you to know that you are not alone.*"

I think I expected something to emerge along the lines of heartfelt discussions talking about our respective grief. That did not happen. We are both men after all, and we are both engineers. What did happen was much more valuable. After a few weeks had passed, Trevor called me into a conference room with a question: "*How long did you and your wife wait after your miscarriage before you started trying to get pregnant again?*" Like me, Trevor had been reluctant to let anyone suffer from being his child. And like me, the first pregnancy had given him a dream. It was hurt in the miscarriage. But he was beginning to dream again.

Some time later, Trevor came into the office one morning visibly shaken. I pulled him into a conference room to ask what was wrong. He told me his wife was six weeks pregnant, and that she had just started bleeding. I told him that your mom had spotted with Elise and Charis at six weeks. We had learned that spotting in early pregnancy is common. The only people who see it as a warning sign are those who have had it end in miscarriage. The agonizing thing about spotting at six weeks if you are concerned is that there is nothing you or the medical professionals can do. You simply have to wait two or three weeks and come back for another ultrasound. I felt incredibly powerless as Trevor described his sense of helplessness, his frustration that a healthy ultrasound at nine weeks still meant three more weeks of waiting to finish the first trimester, his inability to focus his mind on anything else, and yet at the same time the debilitating results from spending all his time wondering what would happen. I had no words of wisdom or solutions to give him. All I could say was that, *"I know how you feel. That is also my story."*

As we sat in the conference room on that day, and on many days following, I told him more of my story. Many times, his response was *"I'm sorry. That really stinks."* Much of what we talked about during those six weeks is what I wrote in the second letter.

> You can't control what happens to the baby, but you can control your response to this time of uncertainty. You and your wife need to find ways to laugh. Don't let the fear grind your lives to a halt. Your wife needs your support. It's okay to feel out of control.

I honestly don't know who was helped more. I stopped talking about the miscarriages after the second letter because I thought I was done processing. By letting me enter into his own uncertainty, Trevor gave me a safe space to remember my experiences again. Those conversations helped me begin talking to your mom. Sometimes I told her what Trevor and I discussed. Other times, my discussion with Trevor initiated a specific conversation with her.

> I realized when Trevor and I talked this morning that you were either pregnant or miscarrying for 18 months before Elise was born. I had not realized the physical and emotional toll that took on you. I'm sorry. And I'm sorry for not being able to support you better because I was wrapped up in my own grief.

Trevor helped me remember. Through that, he helped your mom and I remember together.

The Miscarriages in Our Family— the Open Hand

Our decision to try and "redemptively remember" the miscarriages has become intertwined with the symbol of the open hand. This symbol has been foundational in our marriage, especially at times when we have committed to face unknown circumstances together. It was woven into our decision to date, and later to get engaged. When I asked your mom to marry me, I told her that "*I am finding something beautiful in my life. Will you be part of the journey with me?*" This symbol carries with it a tension we face as firstborns, trained in the sciences, who want to be in control. The tension says that I want to be in control, but I will hold my hand open. It also says that I want to withdraw and protect myself from pain, but I will engage. Through these tensions the open hand helps us move from fear to freedom.

With baby #1, the symbol of the open hand gave us beauty. As we moved from fear to freedom, we laughed with each other about the "extreme sport" of pregnancy and looked forward to the extreme sport of parenthood. That pregnancy gave us the freedom to voice dreams to ourselves and to each other about what life with children could bring us.

With baby #2, the open hand helped me to overcome my anger. I so desperately wanted to make my love conditional on your life not ending with a miscarriage. The open hand told me that "*if you do not open your hand, you will kill what you claim you love.*"

With Elise and Charis, we chose the open hand as an act of discipline. Part of this was a response to the first two miscarriages. We intentionally viewed your lives as gifts from God. We wanted to give God the two lives that, after the two miscarriages, we thought we would never have. At your baptisms, we used the same words from the prayer of farewell in my first two letters.

> Into your hands, O merciful Savior, we give you this child, whom you have given to us. Acknowledge, we pray you, a sheep of your own fold, a lamb of your own flock, a sinner of your own redeeming. Receive this child into the arms of your abiding mercy, into the rest of your everlasting peace, into the glorious company of those who dwell in your light.

The open hand has also called me to fully enter into the relational risk of parenthood with my living children. There are days that I feel inadequate as a father. The open hand calls me to be present in your lives. Folk tales in the US tend to portray fathers as absent, buffoons, or both. You will grow up reading and watching these folk tales. The open hand challenges me to live out a different model of fatherhood, in which I am an active part of your lives, and where my response to feeling inadequate as a father is to still choose relationship with you instead of distancing myself. The open hand also gives me a dream of the joys I can find through this extreme sport called parenting. My relationships with you have lowered the reserve that I feared in my first letter. I have learned to laugh and play with you in ways that I never would have imagined. Through this you have given me the dual joys of watching you grow, and discovering sides of myself that I didn't know existed.

With baby #5, the open hand helped us overcome bitterness. Much of our decision to try and become pregnant again involved whether or not we would "batten down the hatches" around our family of four, and try to control how our lives unfolded. We chose to be open to the uncertainty that another life would bring. When we lost that life in the miscarriage, we decided that our underlying decision would remain. We will bring others into our home, even if we can never have more children. Maybe it will be friends of our living children who need a home for an afternoon when their mother is sick. Maybe it will be children of our adult friends who need a home when their parents are under stress. Maybe it will be an adult friend. The point is that we decided we would intentionally open our lives and our home.

When we decided to try and get pregnant, I prepared myself by saying that another miscarriage would end our efforts to have children. When the miscarriage happened, I found myself seeing death in several other areas of my life. I wanted to simply give up. The open hand helped me talk with your mom about how we could make your death not be the end of the story. Because the miscarriage happened so quickly, your mom didn't have to have a D&C. That meant that our window of opportunity for having another child before she turned 35 was still open. We agreed to approach that window without bitterness. We could choose not to try and get pregnant again. But we had to do so without a bitter sense of "*That's it. We're done.*" We could also choose to try and get pregnant again.

But we had to do so without a bitter sense of "*We've got to have this baby to replace the one we just lost.*"

Through those discussions, we began to name the hope that another life could hold for us. Your mom said to me at one point that "*Our first two 'collaborations' have been so much fun. I would love another chance to see what happens.*" I had tears in my eyes as I replied that "*Kristine, I haven't heard you talk that way since our first pregnancy.*" During the previous December and January, your mom had a couple weeks where she felt under the weather. We had joked with each other that "*maybe you're pregnant.*" We didn't joke like that with Elise and Charis. I think we didn't believe *getting* pregnant indicated anything. But we were able to joke with you. And I think it's because, as the discussions after your death helped us realize, we were starting to name the hope of new life. You gave us that gift, little one.

With Clare, the open hand helped us shine light into the darkness of pregnancy. We approached the entire pregnancy with both Elise and Charis as a "cringe and bear it" period. We treated each milestone as a source of anxiety. The positive pregnancy test meant that we could have another miscarriage. In fact, our first ultrasound for Charis was a Friday night visit to the emergency room when your mom started spotting at 6 weeks. We called my family on the way home to say that "*we just left the emergency room, and we got to see the baby's heartbeat.*" Charis's sixteen week ultrasound showed a placenta previa. Although it ultimately grew out, it restricted your mom's physical activity for the rest of the pregnancy. The twenty-four week mark of viability is when your mom starts seeing newborns in the neonatal ICU. She sees first hand all the things that can go wrong if a baby is born then.

With Elise and Charis, we simply accepted these fears. I'm not sure we realized they were there. We began to name them as we realized that beyond the immediate pain of death, the miscarriages had also cast a dark cloud over how we approached pregnancy altogether. We didn't want that to happen with Clare. Part of this was to try and protect our own mental health. But part of it was that as much as a 5 and 2 yr old could, we wanted Elise and Charis to understand that pregnancy doesn't have to be a nine-month long period of discouraged perseverance.

So we began to name the hope. Initially, all we could hope was that we wouldn't be eternally afraid. That was my request for prayer one Sunday shortly after the 16 week ultrasound. "*These next weeks have been traditionally periods of darkness for us. I don't know if they can become truly joyful, but I just don't want to live under that despair.*" In L'Engle's story, evil loses some of its power when we name it, even though it is still evil. That was my experience here. There was some value in identifying that darkness.

We named the passive hope–*I don't want to be afraid.* That helped us to name our active hope. Elise and Charis added strength to our conversations from the fifth miscarriage. They were living proof of what our "collaborations" could look like. We used them to anticipate what completing the pregnancy would bring. That helped us look forward to meeting you.

The fear of pregnancy never completely disappeared. Your mom, especially, lived with it in a real way. She carries both physical and emotional scars from the miscarriages (as opposed to mine, which are only emotional). We named you Clare, which means *beautiful light.* You were a beautiful light for us through the pregnancy. You helped us begin naming our fear, and then naming an alternate narrative of hope.

The Miscarriages in Our World– Humanity's Wounds

That alternate narrative of hope is the foundation for how we are trying to own our grief redemptively. At the end of my first letter, I was skeptical that I could respond to my grief with an enlarged capacity to enter into humanity's sufferings. At the end of the second letter I began to see how it might unfold. In the last part of this letter, I want to articulate what this has tangibly looked like for your mom and I.

I had dinner after the second miscarriage with Chris, a close friend and co-worker. During that meal, I voiced some of my frustration at what I had learned about how miscarriages were treated. The fact that they were so common, and yet no-one ever told us they could happen (all we heard from family and co-workers was the "when are you going to have kids" question); the fact that such limited research attention was focused on understanding why they occurred, and what, if anything, could be done to prevent them; the collective *"we don't talk about that"* response that left your mom and I feeling like we were being shunned for somehow being inadequate as humans. Chris had an understanding look in his face as he said to me quietly, "*I know how you feel. I've watched my mom battle many of the same dynamics in her work with tuberculosis patients.*"

That conversation was a turning point for me. I didn't think I was bitter after the first miscarriage. I was becoming bitter after the second miscarriage,. My words to Chris justified that bitterness to myself by claiming that the world was ignoring me and my pain. Chris's words helped me see that I was not alone.

I've already mentioned the fact that although we understood conceptually that miscarriages *could* occur, we didn't know they were so common. When they did happen, part of our response was a sense of *"this isn't supposed to happen."* That was complicated by the fact that we didn't actually know *when* each miscarriage took place. With the first one, the ultrasound showed a small embryo without a heart rate, we had the miserable night before the D&C, and then we had the D&C. The death was some time between the ultrasound and the D&C, but it had actually started before the ultrasound. Maybe with the spotting? Maybe even earlier? We didn't know. With the second miscarriage, the final ultrasound showed a sac already breaking up. The D&C removed the dead fetus, but the death occurred some time before that. This was particularly disturbing for your mom. *"I was walking around with something dead inside my body, and I didn't know it."*

We wanted to respond to the miscarriages by finding the factors we could control to explain why they occurred. The doctors told us not to do this. They said the miscarriages were random events. But we wanted something we could isolate–something we could say *"if we do this differently, the miscarriages won't re-occur."* Could it have been the caffeine in our diet? Could it have been your mom's stress at work? Should she not have jogged when we thought she might be pregnant? Should she not have jogged once we knew she was pregnant? We often spent time talking about what-if scenarios for your mom. But could there have been something I did? I resented the times we assumed the miscarriages happened because of something in your mom's body. I wanted a way for flawed sperm to be a reason for your deaths. And I found that I used the term *flaw* intentionally. I didn't want to say that *"this just happened."* I wanted to say *"this happened because we did something wrong."* Because if we did something wrong, then we could learn from our experience, get it right, and avoid another miscarriage.

We learned one reason why searching for controllable factors was a bad idea. We couldn't find them. None of the ideas we came up with made any plausible sense. Our efforts to isolate a factor associated with one of us frequently turned into self-flagellation that claimed we were flawed people because of what happened. That created significant mental stress. Our discussions also created significant relational stress in our marriage. We often disagreed about which factors even merited discussion, much less which ones might actually have any causal power. In our disagreement, we would often lash out at each other in anger. *"Kristine, the doctor said this happens for reasons we don't understand. I hate seeing what you're doing to yourself by trying to make it your fault. You've got to let it go."* Not surprisingly, that lashing out often

did more harm then good. I wanted to solve her pain.
She needed me to reassure her that I loved her even if
something in her body truly did cause the miscarriages.

I couldn't articulate these experiences when I
was thinking specifically about the miscarriages. I
began to understand them after my discussion with
Chris when I started seeing the parallels to events at
work (the *Rituals of the Silent* that I discussed in the
second letter). The recently cancelled new programs
were like the new lives your mom and I had hoped
to see grow to maturity. The tensions between your
mom and I were like tensions that my coworkers
experienced as they tried to work together in the
aftermath of the cancellations, and in the presence
of strong disagreements about why the programs
were cancelled or if they even should have been. The
specific factors were not the same, but the extreme
desire to isolate something to control was very similar.

I pursued these parallels because I needed help.
I couldn't find resources to help me process the
miscarriages. I could find resources that helped me
understand what was going on in the office. My
coworkers were willing to talk about the cancellations,
and I could see how to use these discussions as
research material for my PhD. I also thought that
pursuing those resources might illuminate the
parallels to help me work through the miscarriages.

I said at the beginning of this letter that your mom
and I needed time to process our experiences of the
miscarriages, and time to figure out how to articulate
them to each other. It took several years for us to begin
translating these connections from concepts into a

shared narrative that affects how we live our lives. Let me tell you the elements that have emerged so far.

First, we will encourage those who, like we did, respond to chaos by trying to exert more control over the unknown. We have learned not to respond by telling our friends to learn to live with an open hand. That is what I tried to say to your mom during the second miscarriage. I am blessed that she has forgiven me. When we talk with our friends now, we tell them that "*we understand what it is like face a world that you can't control, and how scary that can feel.*" Your mom is much better at this type of relational encouragement than I am. One of her friends recently wrote the words below to her in an e-mail.

> I'm tired of putting on a happy face and trying to be optimistic and reassuring people around me that he's going to be okay. I'm thankful that we haven't lost our son altogether, but I'm so stinkin' frustrated! That's probably more than you wanted, but I feel like you won't put me down or try to give me a quick-fix phrase or throw "God won't give you more than you can handle" at me. I'm so sick of hearing that. It sure feels like more than I can handle.

Second, we will look for ways to grant dignity to those who, like us, often feel shunned for not achieving the perfection that they or others expect. Pregnancy is much closer to the limits of human existence than we'd realized when we called parenting an extreme sport. But we come across large and small dreams in all sorts of areas of our lives. We will encourage people we cross paths with that it is okay to not be perfect. More importantly, if you are going to have big dreams that involve pushing the limits of what's been done, not seeing those dreams come true in the way you would have expected doesn't mean that you're a flawed person. Part of being human is being fallible, and we live in a broken world. Let's help each other step into those dreams, encourage the hopes for what could be, and mourn the loss of what might have been if the dreams go different directions than we'd hoped.

Part of that encouragement involves finding ways to continue dreaming. We will, as much as we can, respond by saying that death is not the end of the story. I wrote in the lament for baby #5 about facing the choice between *it's over* and *the dream lives.* Your mom and I decided we would work together to keep our dream of an open home alive. Like our discussions during the second miscarriage, the decision to live with an open home was largely independent of whether we did or didn't get pregnant again. In that sense, we said that death wouldn't be the end of the story. We would hold on to the dream.

I've seen this same decision faced repeatedly in the places where I work. I've worked on programs in the aerospace and energy industries that frequently use cutting edge technology that has limited precedent. When precedent exists, the specific products are incredibly complex. This work occurs in organizations that are trying to work in new ways–being agile when they're used to being slow and bureaucratic, or sharing work across locations and countries that are used to working alone. Like pregnancy, these dreams put us at the limits of what we understand how to do. Many times, the results aren't what we wanted. Programs are shut down. Alignment efforts reveal deep-seeded divisions that outlast the person who championed them. Here is an example, taken from a discussion I had with a colleague in 2009.

> Kevin: "I came over here to build a department capability. All I have to show for it is a quiet return to the U. K. after spending 3 months planning office moves."

> My response: "Kevin, our department learned how to do new product introduction on the program you led. Without that program and the skills we learned because of your leadership, the new program that's getting all the department attention right now wouldn't exist. You did start the growth of a capability."

We must choose what we do with our dreams when we face these unexpected outcomes. We can let them die. Or we can find ways to keep them alive. We can decide that the dream was worth reaching for, even if the path of pursuing it hurt more than we would have wanted. That was the crux of my encouragement to Kevin. His dream of a department capability was going to take shape despite the death of the specific program he had come to the U. S. to lead.

When baby #1 died, I read Wolterstorff's words as a challenge. I should be able to help heal humanity's wounds because of what I've been through. Writing this letter has helped me understand that this is only part of the story. I have received healing as I've become open to humanity's wounds. I've learned that I'm not alone in my grief. Engaging in suffering elsewhere has helped me to better understand and engage my own. Now I understand Wolterstorff's challenge a little better. That engagement must be two-way. If I'm not alone in my experience of death, then I need to be willing to see the life, death, and grief in the many places around me. I also need to tell my story. So that the hurting people in those places of death around me will know that they are not alone. And so that, when circumstances permit like they did with Trevor and Kevin, we can help each other live through those encounters without letting death be the final word.

Facing the Future Together

As has become my tradition in writing these letters, I will close again with a text that has been particularly meaningful as I think about all I have written here. We first heard Fernando Ortega shortly after moving to Indianapolis when Pandora played him on my Phil Keaggy station. Your mom listened to this song for encouragement during several months of studying for a challenging pharmacy board certification exam. The words of two friends walking together into the uncertain future symbolized our commitment to each other after the third miscarriage. We would "hold on and help one another" when our burdens became too great to bear. This was a significant change from the separate grieving we did after the first two miscarriages.

The song can also be sung between a father and his children. All six of you walked an uncertain road with me as you have borne my burdens through the words of these letters. You will walk that road with me into the future. My unborn children, each of your presence in our lives continues to shape how your mom and I engage our world. You have challenged us to grant you dignity, and encouraged us to not let your deaths be the last word. Elise, Charis, and Clare, you are calling us into the joy of making new life grow. You will learn with us what it means to remember your three siblings, to live with open hands, and to see and speak peace into humanity's wounds. So we will walk together, until the day when we all meet for the first time.

TAKE HEART MY FRIEND[2]

Take heart, my friend. We'll go together, this uncertain road that lies ahead. Our faithful God has always gone before us, and He will lead the way once again.

Take heart, my friend, we can walk together. And if our burdens become too great, we can hold up and help one another. In God's love, and God's grace.

Take heart my friend. The Lord is with us, as He has been all the days of our lives.
Our assurance every morning; our defender in the night.

If we should falter, when trouble surrounds us; when the wind and the waves are wild and high, we will look away to Him who ruled the waters; who spoke His peace into the angry tide.

He is our comfort, our sustainer. He is our help in time of need. And when we wander, He is our shepherd. He who watches over us never sleeps.

Take heart my friend. The Lord is with us, as He has been all the days of our lives.
Our assurance every morning; our defender in the night.

6

—

EPILOGUE

Songs of Comfort

I wrote in the first letter that I had come to see the role of faith was not to answer the "why" (in this case explaining why the miscarriage happened). Rather, it was to help me find a voice to articulate my emotions. Articulating those emotions enabled me to face my despair and disappointment without letting it become the final word from the miscarriages. These songs represent that process for Kristine and me after the third miscarriage. Expressing our pain, despair, and confusion to each other through these songs helped us to grieve both alone and together. That commitment to grieve together was the foundation for how we responded to the third miscarriage, our decision to try and get pregnant again, and the uncertainty of Clare's pregnancy. I have included these songs as a resource. Kristine and I have written short explanations for particular songs that are meaningful.

Psalm 35—Contend (Sons of Korah)

I (Kristine) have listened to this a lot on my commute to work when it was difficult or I felt challenged by someone. God is the perfect person to complain to! He will always be just to each person.

Psalm 51—A Broken Spirit and a Contrite Heart
(Sons of Korah)

Big Enough (Chris Rice)

The miscarriages were challenges that Kristine and I couldn't overcome by solving problems or answering questions. We needed the encouragement from this song that it is okay to live with unanswered questions.

Hear Me Calling, Great Redeemer (Fernando Ortega)

This is such a powerful lament. We can be honest about our own need because we have a great Redeemer who also suffered on the cross.

Sing Your Praise to the Lord (Rich Mullins)

This song was important after our second miscarriage. It was good for us to acknowledge God is God, with the right to be praised even when we are feeling sad. It was healing for me (Kristine) to play this song while lying face down on the floor in a physical act of worship.

Tear Out My Heart (Brother Sun)

Desert Rose (White Heart)

I (Kristine) listened to this song a lot in 7th grade! It helped as I tried to find my own identity and often felt lonely.

Lay It Down (White Heart)

I (Shawn) had an arrangement of this song from a group at my high school that I listened to many times during my lonely years at Purdue.

We Are Not As Strong As We Think We Are (Rich Mullins)
Again, this was helpful following our miscarriages. Truly,
we are dust of the field. Each breath is from God. The next
two songs reflect this theme.

Part the Waters Lord/ I Need Thee Every Hour (Selah)

Lord of Eternity (Fernando Ortega)

A Communion Blessing from St. Joseph's Square (Rich Mullins)
I (Kristine) listened to this song in my very, very stressful
third year of pharmacy school. It always helped me feel a
little calmer.

Lift Up Your Eyes (The Crossing)
This song was important for our family during our move
to Indianapolis with the uncertainty regarding housing,
a new pregnancy, finding a daycare, and adjusting to new
jobs. It is Charis's song.

I Will Praise Him Still (Fernando Ortega)

Planting a Garden (The Crossing)
This writer wrote this song in response to her own miscarriage.
It was inspired by a man with AIDS who planted a garden.
The idea is that it is worth it to do something good even if
you won't personally see the results.

Someone Who Knows Your Name (The Crossing)
I (Kristine) have such special memories of my year in
Scotland. Such a beautiful land with quite the tragic history.

Mourning Into Dancing (The Crossing)

Healer of My Soul (John Michael Talbot)

The arrangement on *Brother to Brother* (with Michael Card) was another important song for me (Shawn) during my lonely years at Purdue. It became my prayer after our third miscarriage. The next four songs voice different themes on this need for healing and peace.

Jesus, King of Angels (Fernando Ortega)

Hold Me Jesus (Rich Mullins)

Jesus Draw Me Ever Nearer (Margaret Becker / Keith Getty)

This is Elise's song. We sang it a lot when faced with the uncertainty of childbirth and being new parents. We also sang it to her a lot when she wasn't sleeping much!

Sleepless Night (Fernando Ortega)

I Will Lie Down and Sleep (Steve Green)

We sing this song for Elise when she wakes up with bad dreams and for Charis every night before bed. With the next five songs, it builds on David Adam's images of Christ before, beneath, and behind us.

O the Deep, Deep Love of Jesus (Selah)

If I Stand (Rich Mullins)

Peace (Praise & Worship - Lionel Petersen)

Before the Throne of God Above (Selah)

In Christ Alone (Keith Getty / Stuart Townend)
This is Charis's baptism song

Voice of Truth (Casting Crowns)

This was a good song for me as I (Kristine) struggled to fill big shoes in my new position at St Vincent. Both of us tend to hear dominant voices about our inadequacies. We needed to hear the voice of truth during the miscarriages. We are also trying to speak that voice of truth into lives around us.

Joyful, Joyful, We Adore Thee (The African Children's Choir)

The joy of life from our living children has been important for both of us as we've faced our fears and inadequacies as parents, as well as the darkness of miscarriage and pregnancy. It was fitting to include this song, sung by children who have also faced into many of life's darkest areas.

Take Heart, My Friend (Fernando Ortega)

This is a current personal favorite. The words just seem written for me (Kristine). For me (Shawn), it is an anthem for walking forward from the third miscarriage together with Kristine instead of both alone.

New Day (Robbie Seay Band)

This is a song of hope when it is hard to find the courage to look for the positive in a new day.

Forever (Chris Tomlin)

Our church ensemble performed this song shortly after our third miscarriage. It was our family's rallying cry that we would not let the third miscarriage send us into a canyon of despair. It voiced our commitment not to live under the same cloud of fear during Clare's pregnancy that we had while pregnant with Elise and Charis. It is Clare's baptism song.

SOME RESOURCES

Writing this book has helped me find other resources for those who grieve. I've included a short list here of ones that I found particularly helpful.

BOOKS

Brokering, H. *To Henry in Heaven.* Augsburg Fortress, 2005

Cooney, A. T. and Gamino, L. A. *When Your Baby Dies: Through Miscarriage or Stillbirth.* Augsburg Books, 2002

Gilbert, K. R. and Smart, L. S. *Coping With Infant or Fetal Loss: The Couple's Healing Process.* Brunner/Mazel Pub. Company, 1992

Landsman, G. "Does God Give Special Kids to Special Parents?" in L. Layne (ed.), *Transformative Motherhood: On Giving and Getting in a Consumer Culture.* NYU Press, 1999.

Layne, Linda. *Motherhood Lost: A Feminist Account of Pregnancy Loss in America.* Routledge, 2002

O'Neill-White, Siobhan and White, David. *We Lost Our Baby,* Liffey Press, 2007

Schwiebert, Pat. *We were gonna have a baby, but we had an angel instead,* Grief Watch, 2003

Schwiebert, Pat and DeKlyen, Chuck. *Tear Soup: A Recipe for Healing After Loss,* Grief Watch, 1999

Wolterstorff, Nicholas. *Lament for a Son.* Eerdman's Publishing Company, 1987

WEBSITES

http://www.aplacetoremember.com
http://fathersgrievinginfantloss.blogspot.com
http://www.griefwatch.com
http://www.miscarriageassociation.org.uk/
http://www.nationalshare.org/
http://www.uk-sands.org/
http://www.silentgrief.com
http://step.bethany.org/
http://www.wintergreenpress.com

SONGS

Selah (You Deliver Me)—I will Carry You;
    Curb Records, 2009

Watermark (All Things New)—Glory Baby;
    Rocketown Records, 2000

George Canyon (One Good Friend)—My Name;
    Universal South, 2004

Nick and Anita Haigh (Celtic Roots & Rhythms: Heartcry)—
    Song for Kim; Kennedy International Music, 2000

NOTES

Chapter 1: Letter to My First Child

1. Miller, C., *A Requiem for Love* (Dallas, TX: Word Publishing, 1989), pg 148.

2. Wolterstorff, N., "The Grace that Shaped My Life." In Clark, K. J. (ed) *Philosophers Who Believe* (Downers Grove, IL: Inter Varsity Press, 1997), pg 274.

3. Wolterstorff, N., *Lament for a Son* (Grand Rapids, MI: Eerdman's Publishing Company, 1987), pg 71.

4. If We Never Meet Again. Albert E. Brumley. © 1945 Renewed 1973 Stamps Quartet Music/BMI (admin. by ClearBox Rights). All rights reserved. Used by permission.

Chapter 2: Lament - On the Death of My Second Child

1. Wolterstorff, N., *Lament for a Son* (Grand Rapids, MI: Eerdman's Publishing Company, 1987), pg 106-107.

2. Ibid, pg 108, 110-111.

3. Hard to Get. Rich Mullins © 1998 Liturgy Legacy Music (admin. by Word Music, LLC) and Word Music, LLC. All rights reserved. Used by permission.

4. Adam, D., *The Cry of the Deer* (Harrisburg, PA: Morehouse Publishing, 1989), pg 128-129.

5. Ibid, pg 130-131

6. Buechner, F., *Wrestling in the Dark: ABC Theologized.* (San Francisco, CA: Harper & Row, 1988), pg 100.

NOTES

Chapter 3: Letter to My Second Child

1. Lewis, C. S. *Till We Have Faces*, (San Diego, CA:Harcourt Brace & Company, 1980), pg 264.

2. Ibid, pg 291-292

3. LeFevre, P. D. (Ed), *The Prayers of Kierkegaard* (Chicago, IL: University of Chicago Press, 1956), pg 42.

4. Buttrick, G. A., *Prayer* (New York, NY: Abingdon-Cokesbury Press, 1942), pg 260.

5. Ibid, pg 261.

6. Ibid, pg 261-262.

7. Ibid, pg 262-263.

8. Ibid, pg 263.

9. If We Never Meet Again. Albert E. Brumley. © 1945 Renewed 1973 Stamps Quartet Music/BMI (admin. by ClearBox Rights). All rights reserved. Used by permission.

Chapter 4: Lament - On the Death of My Fifth Child

1. Adapted from prayers for "The Shadow of Death" in Northumbria Community's *Celtic Daily Prayer* (New York, NY: HarperCollins, 2002), pg 227. Used with permission.

2. Ibid, pg 222.

3. Ibid, pg 222.

Chapter 5: Letter to My Six Children

1. Tolkien, J. R. R. *The Silmarillion*, (London, UK:The Folio Society, 1997), pg 18.

2. Take Heart My Friend. Fernando Ortega and John Andrew Schreiner. © 2004 Ceredo Verde Music, Curb Songs, and John Andrew Schreiner Music. All rights reserved. Used by permission of Alfred Music Publishing Co., Inc.

ABOUT THE AUTHOR

Dr. Shawn Collins grew up in Kenya as a missionary kid. This cultural diversity built a foundation which influenced his faith and vocation. As a Christian he merges influences from multiple Protestant traditions, including nondenominational, Lutheran and Presbyterian. His work in the aerospace and energy industries integrates graduate degrees in mechanical engineering (M. S.) and anthropology (PhD). He regularly writes and presents on a variety of systems engineering, organizational behavior, and theology topics. *Letters to My Unborn Children* reflects how engineering, anthropology, theology, and his foundational years in Kenya all impact his experiences of grief and suffering. Dr. Collins lives in Indianapolis with his wife and 3 living children.

Shawn founded **Tembea Pamoja, LLC**, in 2012 to manage the publishing and distribution of *Letters to My Unborn Children*. *Tembea pamoja* is a Kiswahili term meaning walk together. It symbolizes the commitment he and Kristine made to integrate the miscarriages into their lives. It also symbolizes the hope that *Letters to My Unborn Children* will encourage others who grieve. You are not alone. We can walk together.

For more information about the book, or to hear
a recording of the Caim Prayer song, please visit:
http://www.letterstomyunbornchildren.com